9/11

THAT BEAUTIFUL, BROKEN DAY

D1564765

Edited by Ellen E. Kennedy

Once upon a time
I lived in a snow globe.
It was a peaceful time and place.
There was snow, but it wasn't cold.
Birds sang, flowers bloomed,
People were happy.

Then one day,
One fateful day,
Planes crashed into my glass dome
And shattered it to pieces.
Instead of snow,
Ash
Was now falling from the sky.
Jagged pieces of glass lay in a heap.
People cried as their world,
Like mine,
Shattered,
Never to be the same again.

Linda Loegel

Table of Contents

INTRODUCTION

It was in the summer of 2020 when our youngest member, Emily Dykstra, mentioned that it would be nineteen years since the momentous 2001 attack on our country. "What if we put together a book of our thoughts and impressions of 9/11 in time for the twentieth anniversary?"

The members of our group, the NC Scribes, responded with enthusiasm. After all, we are all writers, in varying stages of our careers and in varying genres, learning and being inspired by one another to polish our work. We've been meeting on a weekly basis for over eight years now and strong, loving friendships have been formed, based mostly on our shared Christian faith.

September 11, 2001 is one of those "Where were you when you heard?" events. Most of us in the NCS are of retirement age, so the Kennedy assassination is the one we remembered most. For our parents, it was Pearl Harbor. But 9/11 trumps them all for shock, anger, tragedy and fear.

The authors in our group have written true stories, essays and poems that reflect a wide variety of emotions, insights and perspectives. It is our hope that this book will inform subsequent generations of the impact that that event had on everyday Americans.

This book is the result of an inspired—if paradoxical—suggestion, put forth by a young woman whose memories of September 11, 2001 are gleaned mostly from family retelling and photographs. I think, however, that you will find that Emily's story, given pride of place at the beginning of this book, is well-told and well worth telling.

"When things are scary, look for the helpers," the beloved Mr. Rogers said, quoting the sage advice of his mother. And it is to all those who helped, during and after that terrible day, that this book is dedicated. Thank you.

— Ellen E. Kennedy, Editor

FROM HISTORY TO REALITY

I listened to my parents sing along to the radio. I sat in my car seat, kicking my legs and joining in when I could. We were going home on an airplane today, but first, we would visit the animals at the zoo. I hugged my toy elephant to my chest excitedly.

Suddenly the music stopped, right in the middle of a song, and a man's voice replaced it, saying, "We have received unconfirmed reports of an airplane crashing into one of the Twin Towers." Daddy changed the station, and music started playing again, but then it, too, suddenly stopped, as another newscaster announced, "Unconfirmed reports are coming in of an aircraft flying into one of the Twin Towers."

My parents listened closely to the radio, and I stayed quiet. The air felt different, kinda heavy and scary, like a monster had got in the car, too.

My parents parked along the side of the road and waved to my grandparents and uncle, who were in other cars. They soon pulled over too. Mommy and Daddy got out to talk to the other grown-ups.

They left me in my seat. I looked at my dinosaurs and my elephant; they looked scared. "Mommy and Daddy will fix it," I promised them.

My parents got back in the car, and Daddy started driving. The man on the radio began talking again. I listened, hoping he could tell me what was wrong. He kept saying things about airplanes, but I didn't understand what about planes would make Mommy and Daddy's faces look the way they did.

Finally, we got to the zoo. There weren't lots of people there.

My cousins had come, too, with Grandma and Grandpa. Daddy had to stay somewhere to talk on the phone, but the other grown-ups took us kids to visit the animals. They said later we could ride the carousel. We went to the lion's house, but they were sleeping (lions are always sleeping). Then we saw some fish (they had black and yellow stripes) and said "hi" to the elephants. We got to see lots of other animals too.

When we went to ride the Merry-Go-Round, Daddy talked to the carousel man, who said, "The President's coming here."

"Let's get out of here." Daddy said to Mommy and the other grown-ups.

"But we're next in line," My older cousin complained.

"Don't worry. You can ride it before we leave." Grandma promised.

Once the man opened the gate, my cousins and I rushed to find an animal to ride. Daddy helped me up onto mine. It was an elephant with a blue and pink saddle. I grinned as the music began, and we started to go around and around.

Once the ride was over, the grown-ups ushered us to the cars. They decided to find food, and once we ate, Daddy started to drive again. It took a long time, and the man on the radio kept talking about airplanes. Maybe he told Mommy and Daddy that we couldn't go home on ours, because when we finally stopped, we were at Grandma and Grandpa's house.

Over the next few days, my mama watched the TV lots. It looked like one of Daddy's scary shows that I wasn't supposed to watch, she kept giving me toys to play with, but I still saw. Daddy kept going to the town to find out when we could get on our airplane and what we were supposed to do with the car. My grandparents had to go back to work.

Mommy told me that some very bad people had done some very bad things.

I wanted to go home, and so did Mommy and Daddy, but the plane people didn't want to take us home, though the car people were being nice and letting us keep our car extra time. Finally, Daddy found out that they weren't making people pay extra money for returning cars to different places, so they borrowed some of Grandma and Grandpa's toys, buckled me in, and started to drive and drive and drive.

It took forever. We had to stop at nights and have adventure sleeps at hotels, but I got to play with my cousins one day, 'cause they lived close to where we had one of our adventure sleeps. I don't get to see those cousins a lot, so that was fun. And one day we went to see some faces on a mountain, but it was foggy, so we couldn't see them.

Then finally we got to our house. We were so happy to be home.

* * *

I scrolled mindlessly through my social media as I listened to music on my phone. It was September 11, so naturally, my feed was peppered with content about the terrorist attack in 2001.

I wasn't really paying attention; I was mostly just

scrolling to keep my hands busy.

It had been nearly two decades since 9/11 and I thought of it much like I thought of the attack on Pearl Harbor, a terrible event one read about in textbooks, far removed from me. I was not even three when the towers fell, and while changes came that rocked the world and no doubt affected me, I was so young that the world before them seems almost like a reverse dystopia. Submitting to security and strict regulations at an airport is simply expected, and the idea that you could ever meet somebody or say goodbye at the gate is nothing short of entirely foreign.

As I continued browsing my feed, one video caught my attention. It was recordings of the final calls the victims of 9/11 made to say goodbye. As I listened to call, after call, after call, I felt tears rolling down my cheeks. For the first time, these people were more than statistics in my mind. More than victims even, they were human beings with emotions, families, and lives who wanted the chance to say and hear "I love you" one last time. I finished the video and thought for a long time. As I began to understand the reality of the tragedy of that day, I felt my heart breaking.

— Emily Dykstra

A SAFE RETREAT?

The weather was near perfect on this September day in New York's Adirondack Mountains. We were vacationing at a cottage on Saranac Lake and decided to take a morning hike through the woods. As we walked down the road, the dappled sunlight showed through the trees, lighting up the forest. We stopped to enjoy wildflowers and listen to bird calls before we continued our walk.

A car traveled down the unpaved road after we had walked a mile or so. It stopped right in front of us. The driver greeted us and asked, "Did you know an airplane crashed into the World Trade Center?"

We looked at each other. What did this tragedy have to do with us? Plane crashes occasionally occur, but why did the stranger think we should be concerned about this one? Why did he urge us to turn on the news? We stared at him as if he were some alien from Mars.

Our curiosity soon got the best of us, and we turned around to go back to the house. We informed other family members we were going to watch the news. Hopefully, we hadn't missed the featured story.

As soon as we turned on the TV, we sat spellbound. The horrific events of the day unfolded before our eyes. The camera surveyed the carnage of the plane crash and the scenes of the burning building. Panicked people were screaming and jumping out of the windows to their deaths. A part of the Tower where the plane had hit was completely gone!

As we sat on our comfortable sofa, we were unable to take our eyes off the TV screen. We couldn't imagine anything worse happening, but then it did. A second plane crashed into the other Tower of the World Trade Center. In the following moments, we heard the words, "Terrorist attack."

A wave of fear washed over us as we realized these crashes were not accidents. Our country was at war! The news coverage of this was continuous, and we stayed glued to our chairs.

More gruesome news: another plane had flown into the Pentagon. Then, as we watched in horror, the two towers of the World Trade Center collapsed. Billows of smoke and toxic fumes saturated the area. People on the ground covered their faces to avoid breathing in the pollution. The fumes darkened the sun and turned the bright day into twilight. A face that looked like the devil appeared in the clouds. The sight was bone-chilling, but the news media quickly removed it from future broadcasts.

Then a different flight, presumed to be headed for the White House, crashed in a field in Pennsylvania. Moments before, people on board phoned to say they were fighting the terrorists. These heroes had succeeded in diverting the plane, but they lost their lives in the resulting crash.

After witnessing the horror show on TV, we gazed out our window. Everything outside the house was peaceful and still. No breeze ruffled the leaves in the trees. The lake was glassy smooth. We breathed in deeply as the serenity of the scene calmed our souls. When we saw the peaceful setting in front of us, the bloodshed on TV seemed unreal. The awful events seemed to be happening in another world, yet they had actually happened in our own country. We could hardly absorb the enormousness of it all.

The terror even overshadowed our peaceful retreat. We later learned that Flight 11 out of Boston's Logan Airport flew over Saranac Lake, piloted by terrorist Mohammed Atta. While the passengers complied with instructions to remain in their seats, the plane flew over the lake, then turned south, ultimately hitting the South Tower. What if they had fought the terrorists and the plane had crashed into Saranac Lake? We might have been right in the middle of a tragic scene.

Now we no longer take our lives for granted. We try to live each day as if it could be our last. After all, you never know. As we found out that September morning, it just might be.

— *Joanne Check*

TIMING

Excitement coursed through my body as I got into the back seat of my sister Betty Jo's car. She and her husband Jerry were flying out of Dulles International Airport near Washington, D.C. that afternoon for a month-long visit with their daughter and her family in Beirut, Lebanon. The plan was for the three of us to drive to D.C. where I would drop them off and then drive their car back to Raleigh, North Carolina.

The enthusiasm was palpable as we started our journey. For me this would be a five-hour ride with them and then a five-hour drive back on roads I have driven many times. I had an audio book in my bag that I would listen to on the way home. We had planned a buffer of time to allow for unexpected traffic or other events. It was 8:40 AM. We were right on time.

The radio played softly in the background, leaving space for the energy that radiated through the air as they spoke of plans for time to be spent with their grandchildren. It had been several months since they had seen them. This highly-anticipated trip had been planned for a long while. I settled into the passenger seat on this leg of their adventure, enjoying their joy. I treasured being able to look out and just experience the scenery.

As we made our way across town to the highway, the music stopped and we heard the announcer say something crazy about a plane hitting one of the Twin Towers of the World Trade Center. My stomach muscles tensed as we turned our attention to the radio. It was 8:50 AM.

All right, uh, Pat, we are just currently getting a look at the World Trade Center.

We have something that has happened here at the World Trade Center.

We noticed flame and an awful lot of smoke from one of the towers of the World Trade Center.

We are just coming up on this scene, this is easily three-quarters of the way up...we are... this is...Whatever has occurred has just occurred, uh, within minutes and, uh, we are trying to determine exactly what that is. But currently we have a lot of smoke at the top of the towers of the World Trade Center, we will keep you posted...

"What did they say? Something about the World Trade Center?" Jerry said, "We're less than a mile from your father's house. Let's go there and watch his TV with him."

Daddy lived in West Raleigh, just off Western Blvd. He was delighted to see us. He turned to my sister and said, "I thought you were off to D.C. for your flight to Lebanon today."

"We were, but hearing the announcement on the radio made us want to know more about what's going on." Jerry went straight to turn on the TV. As it came to life, we saw dark smoke billow out of one side of the tower. "What on earth is happening?"

We hugged each other and sat down to watch. Our puzzlement quickly turned to horror as we saw a second plane hit the second tower within minutes of the first. It was 9:03 AM. We watched people fleeing the towers as rescue workers pushed past them to assist and help with order in the chaos. We could barely believe what our eyes were seeing as people jumped out of windows in the upper stories to a certain death.

"Lord be with us in this crazy time of chaos."

At 9:38 AM, a third plane crashed into the Pentagon and started a violent fire. My muscles turned to rubber as we helplessly watched the flames and pondered what would happen next. "We are under attack."

At 9:45 AM, the United States airspace was shut down.

The announcer on TV said that all flights, domestic and foreign, were cancelled. No planes would be leaving the ground until further notice.

When a fourth plane was hijacked at 9:28 AM, passengers learned about the World Trade Center and Pentagon crashes and resisted the demands of the hijackers. They used their cell phones to tell family and friends they loved them as three passengers planned to breach the cockpit door. When the hijackers learned of their plan, they crashed the plane in a field in Pennsylvania.

At 10:28 AM, we saw the North Tower collapse. Nearly two thousand people were at or above the points of impact. Only eighteen, who were in a staircase that held, were able to escape.

At 11:00 AM, Transport Canada halted all airport departures.

"We are under attack." Jerry said, "I don't think we are going anywhere today."

In disbelief, Betty Jo said, "But we have worked so hard to make this trip happen, I can't imagine NOT going."

"All air traffic is shut down in the United States for

the immediate future. We don't know the full impact of what's happening or when air traffic will open back up."

My heart ached for them as they faced the reality of staying home and letting go of their plans. Inwardly, I thanked God they were safe and that we had not left town.

Jerry called their daughter, Patty, and talked with her husband, Imad. He had heard the news and assumed they would not be able to come.

We spent the day with Daddy as we tried to make sense of what was happening and what its impact on our world would be. I was glad that we had all been together as this day unfolded.

At 5:20 PM, the South Tower collapsed.

At the end of the day, we each went back to our own space and tried to reorient ourselves.

Over the next few days the skies were eerily quiet. Travelers were renting and sometimes buying cars to get back home. I was thankful to be home and not out of town on a business trip far away. Everywhere I went, the plane crashes and their implications were the main topic of conversation.

It was several days before air travel resumed and weeks before we returned to some semblance of normalcy.

The next summer the long-awaited trip took place with lots of fun time with grandchildren.

— Janet Harrison

A DAY NOT TO BE FORGOTTEN

As we approached the beginning of a new century, rumors of Doomsday events ran wild. Y2K, the Millennium Bug, some predicted, would cause computers to crash, thus plunging the world into utter chaos. The year 2000 was projected to be the "beginning of the end" as global catastrophes were to follow and the future of our planet was expected to be grim.

Nervously, we rang in the New Year. Fortunately, the world didn't come to an end and the computers didn't grind to a halt. The forecasted overnight disasters failed to materialize and we seemed to have escaped unscathed, but there was still a sense of concern and trepidation throughout the year.

Three-hundred and sixty-five days later, we again rang in the New Year. With a sigh of relief that the year 2000 was soon to be behind us, we watched a new morning dawn. As a family, we were excited and looked forward to a wonderful year in 2001, jam-packed with important events.

Our winter months were filled with baby showers and anticipation of the birth of our first grandchild. We were over the moon when in March our grandson was born. Nothing could have been more wonderful.

Spring was crammed with wedding showers, bachelor and bachelorette parties. We were busy preparing for our younger daughter's marriage. Family and friends traveled to North Carolina to celebrate the happy occasion and our grandson, Jake, was now three months old. Despite a hurricane having just dumped ten inches of rain the day before, we had a gorgeous morning for an outdoor venue.

We coasted through summer filled with warm memories of a beautiful wedding and overwhelming delight as we watched our grandson grow. It was proving to be one of the best years for our family.

September 11 was a beautiful morning in Rochester, New York. It was an ordinary morning for most. People got ready for work, some boarded planes, others attended business meetings. I was at the dental office where I worked. I was seating a patient in the dental chair when we heard someone scream. My treatment room was closest to the reception area and I bolted through the doorway. The mother of my patient was trembling as she pointed to the television that hung on the wall. What unfolded next was beyond anyone's comprehension.

Like the rest of the world, we were soon glued to the television, watching the news broadcasters relaying information. All dental work ceased. We finally called the rest of the patients and rescheduled every appointment. Sickened by the reports unfolding, we huddled close to each other, trying to find comfort. News footage, in real time, showed the planes crashing into the Twin Towers. We continued to listen and we learned of planes crashing into the Pentagon and in a field in Pennsylvania. Now it was obvious that this was not an accident but an all-out attack on our nation.

That September morning was filled with terror. Real

heroes were born and thousands lost their lives. Emergency responders rushed to the scene to rescue people. We watched in disbelief as the towers collapsed onto themselves. We knew many people were trapped. The hospitals prepared for the injured, but they never came. It was an unprecedented attack on American soil, the likes of which we had never experienced, and I was horrified.

In my state of shock, all I wanted was to hear from my family. I called everyone, but I couldn't reach my newlywed daughter, Christy, who was on a business trip in Boston. Since two flights that were hijacked departed from Logan airport, there was no way to know if Boston was the next target. My new son-in-law was supposed to join her and I feared he was in the air. I was more than distraught.

My boss received a frantic call from his wife. He learned that three members of his family had ties to the World Trade Center that day. It was agonizing, waiting together for news. Communication with anyone in New York City was virtually impossible. It was late in the day when we learned that, at last minute, a regular morning meeting was scheduled to an off-site location, one person spared. Another appointment in the South Tower was canceled, and a morning alarm clock that didn't go off all safeguarded two more people. Prayers for our boss's family were answered.

My husband was babysitting our grandson and remembers hugging him to his chest, not wanting to let him go. He wanted to protect him from these horrible events, wondering what kind of world was in store for this tiny baby. When our daughter, Tracey, came to pick up her son, she told us some friends were at a sidewalk café near the Trade Center when the first plane hit. They sprinted to safety as debris fell from the sky. I was grateful Tracey had decided not to accompany them on that trip. It would have been too much to handle, fearing for the lives of both daughters.

At home, my husband and I still waited, paralyzed with fear, to hear from our daughter in Boston. It was late evening before we connected. When we finally talked, I heard a frightened voice. She told me that several co-workers rented cars and offered her a ride back to North Carolina but since she was the moderator of the conference, she had to stay. She told me she was terrified and regretting her decision. She just wanted to be home with her husband, who was safe because his flight was canceled.

One of my co-workers was on a dream vacation in Alaska. They were dropped off in the wilderness and were to be picked up on September 11. No plane came. For three days, they were panic stricken, without any way to contact the outside world and of course, unaware of the attacks. They later learned their float-plane pilot, oblivious to the terrorism that besieged our nation, attempted to fly to the designated rendezvous point, but was soon diverted by two fighter jets that had been scrambled out of nearby Eielson Air Force Base.

My daughter Christy made it home safely and when she returned to the Boston airport two weeks later, the security was on high alert. She dreaded the flight home and was fearful and uneasy. As she waited at her gate for her flight to be called, Christy was suddenly surrounded by police and airport security. They asked her if she knew the man seated next to her who appeared very fidgety and nervous, clutching a duffel bag. She looked up in alarm, unable to speak, and shook her head. They grabbed her, pushing her to safety. She looked on in horror as they surrounded the suspicious passenger, handcuffed him, and escorted him away. We never heard what happened to him.

The world changed that dreadful day. Like it was for most people, it was filled with worry and prayers. For days and weeks, and even twenty years later, those images are embedded in our memory like it was yesterday. The plumes of smoke and images of people covered with ashes, running for their lives, are as vivid today as on that September 11th. Most of us recall exactly where we were and the personal events that constituted our day. Where were you when the world stood still?

— *Terry Hans*

NEVER TO BE FORGOTTEN

I arrived at my office early to catch up after being out the previous day. I was struggling to find a way to approve the first mortgage application of my workload. The qualifying guidelines for our state's low to moderate-income program for families buying their first house had little flexibility. I knew all too well how elusive the dream of owning that first home could be, and worked diligently to make as many of those aspirations come true as possible.

Unfortunately, the couple's income didn't support the proposed housing expense with their current debt load. As always, it was sad, knowing their dream would have to wait a bit longer. As I began writing up the declination letter, another underwriter stopped at my door.

"Can your family see the smoke?" she asked.

"What smoke?"

"Your family in New York," she explained on seeing my confused look. "A plane crashed into a building in New York. We're in the break room watching it on TV," she said and rushed down the hall. I jumped up to follow her.

The room was packed. It was also completely silent, except for the announcer's solemn voice, filling the room with the horrifying news. By then, the South Tower had also been attacked. Many of us prayed as we watched the burning Twin Towers. It was hard to breathe. I was thankful my parents and the families of my five siblings were over three hundred miles upstate. Our daughters and their families had relocated with us years earlier.

While we were still trying to absorb the atrocity, American Flight 77 hit the Pentagon. The images were overwhelming. Other co-workers arrived. I made room for them by returning to my own one hundred-square-foot office, wondering how this could be real. Needing to embrace normalcy or at least have something positive happen, I flipped this morning's file back open and began reviewing every line of each document.

Then I found it. Just a small thing, which on another day may have gone unnoticed. A discrepancy on the couple's required three years of tax returns caught my eye. Each of them showed three dependent children. Flipping back to the application confirmed only two were listed— ages seven and nine. I dialed the realtor's number to ask about the missing child. The first ring brought a wave of dread. What if the answer held more awful news? Getting her voicemail gave me time to prepare

"Is that loan already approved?" she asked a few minutes later. "We could all use some good news today!"

"Well," I began, not sure I wanted to know the answer. "All three years of their tax returns show three children. But their application shows only two. Please don't tell me something happened to one of them. Not today."

"No," she replied sounding relieved, "that would be his son, Kevin, from his first marriage. The mom couldn't handle a teenage boy after her car accident, so she sent him to live with his dad for a few years. Support payments to the mother probably continued because there was no set agreement of how long he'd be living on this side of town. He moved back when he got accepted to State, which is where most of his old buddies are going too. My daughter's going to miss him. She was at his eighteenth birthday party a few weeks ago."

"Yes. And it shows on his paystub too," I added. "Wait a minute..." I flipped back to verify he was paid monthly. "His employer couldn't stop the deduction because Kevin wasn't eighteen yet!" I exclaimed to myself and the agent. "Once the child support is deleted, I'm positive the loan will meet the requirements, and I'll call the employer for written verification that the deduction is over."

We were both elated. While it was always gratifying to help make a family's dream come true, that day, of all days, it meant so much more.

Driving home that night, there was still disbelief, fear, and anger riding home with me. But that one happy event lessened some of the pain in my heart and I was grateful to have been able to find something good about the day.

Surprisingly, I received a second helping of gratitude that evening. A group text went from one branch of our family tree to the other. My cousin Pat and his family had moved to New Jersey, close to New York, a few years earlier. His son was excited about starting the job he had recently been offered. But the night before the big day, he was informed that the person who would start his training was delayed out of state, so the start date was pushed back two days. I'm sure it was disappointing to the recent college graduate. But the original start date was September 11th, in the Twin

Towers. Without that delay, his brand-new future may have ended before it even started.

For this and all the other miracles of that day, I am eternally grateful.

— Barbara Bennett

OUR FAMILY 9/11

The day was memorable for its very ordinariness. Breezy, sunny and clear, warmish, but not too warm. Just the kind of autumn day I liked best.

Everyone was starting their day: my husband Harold at his R&D office with our son-in-law, David, the CFO of our little company; David's wife, our daughter Laurie, was at the financial office where she was a secretary. Daughter Louise was a senior at Meredith College, working part-time for a home inspector.

And I was at the kitchen table, having my quiet time.

The first indication of a problem was a phone call from Laurie. "Mommy, turn on the television. A plane has hit one of the Twin Towers in New York City!"

After hanging up, I briefly watched the news report. It sounded like an accident, like the one right after WWII, when a small plane hit the Empire State Building. That's how I pictured it. I turned off the TV and returned to my quiet time, saying a prayer for the poor errant pilot and the people who were in the building.

The phone rang again. "Mommy, it's no accident! They've hit the other tower," Laurie said, her voice trembling.

Still on the phone, I turned the TV back on. Now the

reporters sounded much more alarmed. Suddenly, someone announced gravely, "We've just learned that a plane
has hit the Pentagon in Washington." There was video
of a huge fire.

"Oh, no," I murmured, my heart sinking, "We're
really at war!"

Laurie appeared at my doorstep. Her boss was in
Chicago and couldn't use the return airline tickets she'd
arranged for him. Planes were grounded all over the
world. He'd called the office and told everybody to go
home. She came to our house, she said, "Because David
says we should be together."

The news reports were hard to watch. The images
are scrambled in my mind, in no particular order: Smoke
billowing from the two skyscrapers, people falling—or
jumping—to their deaths, the catastrophic collapse. The
report of another plane hijacked over Pennsylvania that
had crashed in an empty field. School children headed
to an awards ceremony were on that plane. The shocked
President being informed of the catastrophe.

"I can't watch anymore," Laurie said. "Let's do
something, go someplace."

For reasons I can't explain, we chose Cary Towne
Center, the nearest mall. Retail therapy, perhaps? There
weren't many people there. The emptiness made me feel
even more bereft. I certainly didn't feel like buying anything. And in the back of my mind, it occurred to me that
a mall would be a good terrorist target.

"Let's go to Joanne's Fabrics," Laurie suggested. On
a good day, we both loved the hobby potential of the
craft store. Today, we purchased red, white and blue rib-
bons. "We can make pins to wear," Laurie said. We had
to do something.

At the office, my husband Harold learned of the

attack from David. They watched events unfold on his computer. When they couldn't take the horror any more, David suggested, "Let's go get some flags!"

They went to a nearby Lowe's home improvement store and bought flags they could mount on their cars. They had to do something. On the way home, Harold remembers, American flags seemed to fly from every car and grace every building.

Our younger daughter Louise heard the news on her car radio. She called her boss, who was in the middle of an inspection and was irritated at being interrupted. A few minutes later, he called her back to apologize. He now understood.

Her husband Sean was stationed in South Korea with the U.S. Army. Was he all right? Her Instant Message went unanswered. Sometime later, he was finally able to call and reassure her of his safety. Apparently, everybody was calling everybody else, all over the world, and it was hard to get through.

More images fill my memory: gray faces, covered with ash. The President standing on the huge mound of debris, promising to find who'd perpetrated the outrage. Our good friend Joanne, a ticket agent for American Airlines, experiencing some harrowing phone calls. Reports of the incredible courage of passengers, pilots and flight attendants, fighting back against the hijackers. Poignant paper flyers stuck on every wall in New York, pleading for any information about missing loved ones.

My husband Harold's elderly sister, living alone in Jacksonville, Alabama, put a huge American flag magnet on her garage door, visible from the street. Like everybody, she had to do something.

Until six months before the attack, my brother Andrew had occasionally worked at an office in the

World Trade Center, but had changed to a new job using new facilities. He was in New York City on the day of the attack for a meeting with attorneys in a mid-town office. He had a clear view of the catastrophe and did what he could to help in all the chaos. He was eventually able to get a train out of the city after the authorities declared the tracks and tunnels safe for travel late that evening.

Our daughter Laurie and her husband David had been invited to visit them in New York and do the tourist things, including a meal at the Windows on the World restaurant atop the North Tower, but fortunately the plans were never realized.

The summer before, Laurie and I had enjoyed being tourists in Washington, D.C., taking in the memorials and other historic spots. We rode past the Pentagon, remarking on the huge size of the building. Little did we realize that just three months later, it would be the scene of such awful devastation.

But for every tragedy that day, there are a dozen stories of rescue and near-misses. Authorities say that out of the 74,280 Americans directly targeted, 93% survived or avoided the attacks.

God's hand was apparent everywhere.

We would be foolish to deny that there is evil in the world, but we can take comfort in the knowledge that the Lord has provided a way to be with Him forever, through Christ.

"Fret not thyself over evildoers," Psalm 37 tells us. And later, in John 16, Jesus echoes, "In the world ye shall have tribulation: but be of good cheer; I have overcome the world."

— *Ellen E. Kennedy*

A MESSAGE TO JACOB

Months after 9/11, in the storage cabinet in my treatment room at the dental office where I worked, I found a folded blue-paper we used as a tray cover. I was astonished when I read its contents. Scrawled in practically illegible handwriting, I had written a poem that day to my infant grandson. That intense love I have for that baby and the panic and despair I felt at that moment, must have inspired me to write my thoughts. I have no memory of composing it, but I added the poem that follows to his baby book.

A Message to Jacob
SEPTEMBER 11, 2001

Jacob, my dearest, the world
has changed today.
A terrorist attack, this morning,
took your safety away.
At six months old,
you now have to worry,
about revenge and retaliation
from an adult's savage fury.

It makes no sense
to harm innocent people.
We all pray to God, under
the church's big steeple.
When you grow up you'll
build hopes and dreams.
Make a difference in this world
of dreadful schemes.

It's hard to understand
when the world is not even safe
for children to play.
When you grow up
to be a big strong man,
we hope your children never
have fear to understand.

Mommy and Daddy will protect you
as much as they are able.
But your mission, in life, is to make
the world more stable.
Your good example
and love of all mankind,
will help the world become a place
where we share a peaceful mind.

— *Terry Hans*

September 11, 2001
FROM A POLICE POINT OF VIEW

September 11, 2001 was the day after my son's twenty-fourth birthday and the start of his second year of med school. That meant his birthday celebration with his mom and me was him running through the house opening his card, pulling out the money, and yelling, "Thanks, Mom and Dad, love you," as he disappeared out the door, slamming it behind him.

My work assignment for that week as a Detective with the Louisville Police Department was teaching a class on interrogation and profiling to some police from small departments located in northern Kentucky. The class was held in Frankfort, about an hour drive from my home in Louisville.

I woke up early on the 11th to a beautiful day, better suited for golf than sitting indoors in a classroom. I recalled that a couple of the officers I had worked with before had mentioned that they were members of a golf course in the area and I could be their guest if we finished class early enough. Since I was the one in charge of that day's agenda, I was confident we would finish in plenty of time for a few holes of golf.

My golf clubs and I were settled in the car and

29

headed for class by 6:30 that morning. The sun was up, and the temperature was about 65 degrees. It was an easy drive down the interstate. I pulled in the police station where the class was to be held in plenty of time to grab morning coffee and steal a donut from the sergeant working the front desk. I then headed down to the classroom to put handouts on their individual desks and wait for my students. Police being police, the class finally got started around quarter after eight. By that time, I had been asked a half-dozen times if I had brought my clubs by various officers trying to plan on an early end to class.

At 8:46 AM that clear Tuesday morning, our lives changed. The lieutenant stepped in the door and without a word, turned the television on. The newsman was announcing in a shocked voice that a Boeing 767 had just crashed into the 96th floor of the North Tower of the World Trade Center in New York City. The facts were not clear right away as to what had happened, when eighteen minutes later a second Boeing 767 appeared in the sky and sharply turned toward the South Tower, hitting it near the 80th floor. We watched as our brother and sister first responders ran toward the explosions and into the buildings, hoping to get as many people out as they could. We all looked at one another helplessly, as we watched our fellow Americans jump out of windows above the explosions to keep from being burned alive.

When lunchtime came, the whole class refused to move from the television, not even to eat. By then, we had witnessed the second plane hitting the South Tower and it was clear that we were being attacked. We watched, horrified, as a third plane hit the west side of the Pentagon at 9:37 AM and a fourth plane was hijacked and went down in a field near Shanksville, Pennsylvania.

We all took turns checking on our loved ones, trying

to reassure them and ourselves, but never getting more than a few feet from the television. One of the uniform cars on the street brought us five pizzas donated by Pizza Hut and sat with us to eat and watch what they had only been hearing about on the radio.

My folks had left the day before, driving out west on a vacation and we had no way of getting in touch with them until they checked in. There was a phone in the car when they bought it, but they had not had it turned on. Dad had decided that since there was a phone booth on every corner, they didn't need one in the car.

The lieutenant decided to close class early, not knowing what would come next. One of the officers asked, "Does this mean we are not playing golf?" using a little police street humor that helped to relieve the tension, and everyone forced a laugh and walked to their cars.

I listened to the radio on my drive back to Louisville and then went to police headquarters, where I found information coming in over the teletype faster than we could read it. Meetings of federal, state, and local law enforcement were ongoing with police from smaller departments meeting in conference rooms of whatever large department was nearby. The airport was closed and the Air National Guard had jets patrolling the skies.

The FBI had issued warnings to watch for large rental trucks parked near public buildings and the courts were closed in order to set up tighter security. Warnings were also out for people to watch for packages left unattended and every radio and television station kept repeating, "If you see something, say something." The news reports stopped showing the planes hitting the Towers and started showing the buildings crumbling to the ground. They began talking about casualties and how many people had not managed to escape. A hot-line number was set up to take calls. All first responders made sure their families were safe, then returned to the job.

The fever on the street was filled with hate for people of Middle Eastern descent. People who had been neighbors and co-workers for years were now the enemy and this hate had to be dealt with, one person at a time.

Everywhere we went as police officers, people wanted to buy us coffee and shake our hand or pat us on the back. It was a time when everywhere we went, folks thanked us for what we did, as if thanking the first responders in New York.

The FBI released information that the terrorists were trained to fly in schools right here in the United States. In the police station teletype room, some of the reporters were waiting for the next report to come in so they could carry the information back out to their coworkers in the hall. One of the reporters showed us footage of President Bush reading to a class of small children as a Secret Service agent whispered in his ear about the attack. The agent took the President by the arm to help him up from the little chair he was sitting in to get him to a place of safety. President Bush pulled his arm back and the agent later reported that the President said he was not going to scare the kids and he would leave when he finished the story.

Mom and Dad eventually called my sister when they stopped for the night and seemed to be the only people in the world that didn't know the events of the day. They had been driving down the road, looking at the sights and talking. My sister asked if they were coming back home to which my dad answered, "No, what can we do?"

Hours became days and days became weeks. The

world watched as first responders searched the rubble for survivors, moving the large pieces of concrete by hand. We heard the stories of the people on the plane that went down in Pennsylvania, having texted or called their families to say goodbye. They believed that the plane was headed for the White House and they were determined to fight back. One wife said she heard her husband yell, "Let's roll," as the passengers tried to take control of the plane back from the terrorists.

I was proud to be a first responder as I watched my brothers and sisters run into the towers to save people they didn't even know. One of the things that frontline people think about as we watch, is would we have had what it took to run into the fire? No matter how many times you do it, you wonder about the next time.

Families getting together with other first responder's families became more important. Police officers' husbands, wives, and children would speak of the sound they wait to hear of Velcro being pulled apart on their loved ones' bulletproof vests that meant they had returned home safe. Life went on, forever changed, and we were grateful for each moment together.

— *James Lewis*

PROTECTING INNOCENCE

So do not fear, for I am with you; do not be dismayed,
for I am your God. I will strengthen you and help you;
I will uphold you with my righteous right hand.
Isaiah 41:10 (NIV)

The name of the Lord is a fortified tower;
the righteous run to it and are safe.
Proverbs 18:10 (NIV)

I cradled my corded phone between my right ear and shoulder, while shaking out a pint-sized shirt from the warm laundry pile on my bed.

"Hi. What?" I couldn't quite grasp what my husband Gordy was saying on the phone. Something about a plane, but he'd just driven out of town on a short business trip in Washington State.

"Turn on the news, it's big. Then call me back," he said.

I turned on our bedroom television and immediately saw the screen filled with an image of the Twin Towers in New York, smoke pouring out of one. Sirens blared. An announcer, standing outside with the towers in the background, spoke with an emotionally choked voice as panicked people ran by him. From his words, it seemed the newsman was scrambling to keep up with ever-changing guesswork about why in the world a plane had hit the North Tower.

Four-year-old Elisa wandered into the room. "Why is smoke on that tower?" She stood stock-still and stared. "Stuff is falling out of those windows."

In horror, I thought, *That's not stuff. That's people. Falling—or jumping.* Out of a one-hundred-and-ten-story building.

I steered Elisa out of the room, casually saying, "How about playing with some Play-Doh?"

"Are people in there? They're high, like Tyler's Lego towers. Is it a movie?"

I just nodded. "Only for grownups to watch. Hey, here's your fun Play-Doh® cookie making toy. What colors do you want?"

As she became engrossed in playing, I slipped away back inside my bedroom and locked the door, so Elisa wouldn't see anything more. I wondered what my older kids, 10-year-old Aimee and 15-year-old Tyler, were hearing or watching at their school. I turned the TV volume down and continued to watch wide-eyed as I called my husband back.

He answered right away. "Ray! Ray works in the North Tower! I think around floor 75. I wonder what's going on?"

Ray was his best friend from high school, from when Gordy had lived in Morristown, N.J. as a teen. Ray had also been a groomsman at our wedding.

Before that, Gordy and I had visited the Twin Towers, dining with his parents in the restaurant at the top on New Year's Eve of 1977. The sparkling city below had been a beautiful sight, and of course we'd taken the elevators, up and down. Now all I could imagine was how far it was from the top of the tower to the ground below. I pictured frantic and injured people crowding into stairwells, inching down those many floors amidst odors of jet fuel and smoke. I shuddered.

Gordy and I agreed to stay in touch and to pray. I went back and forth, from the TV to the kitchen, checking on Elisa. I tried to occupy her with various projects.

Within a few hours, the North Tower had crumbled to a pile of mangled debris. The second tower had been hit too. Terrorism was suspected.

I called Gordy a third time. He could hardly speak, but said, "I'm praying he got out. On the news, I see a lot of people on the street who got out."

Weeks passed, with no word from Ray, despite messages Gordy left on his answering machine. We tried to avoid talking graphically about it or worrying too much about Ray in front of the girls, but were able to speak more honestly in private with our teen son.

After many, many calls to Ray, Gordy finally reached him. He'd indeed gotten out in time, but was traumatized. Ray told us later how he had stood in a very long line at a pay phone trying to reach his wife, hours after the event, to let her know he was alive. Some people had cell phones but the cell phone network was overloaded and interrupted. Ray made his way home and he and his wife had escaped to the country for a while, to get away from the scene. His office was obliterated to dust, anyway. He must have been grieving at the loss of people he knew in that tower. The memories of his escape must have been a nightmare.

Our kids realized something momentous had happened, something life-changing for our country.

American flags hung in front of homes for weeks on end.

As the kids grew, every year on the anniversary of 9-11 the news stations replayed details of that fateful day. At some point, Elisa did of course realize it was people who fell from those windows. I felt sad I could no longer protect her innocence about that. Yet now at age 24, she says she doesn't remember much about it, so I must have in small measure protected her.

The true reality of that day recently hit home for her in a strong way when I loaned her a book about that day. Elisa is a dog lover and owner of a new pup, so I shared with her the story of a man whose seeing-eye dog helped rescue him from one of the Twin Towers.

Thunder Dog: The True Story of a Blind Man, His Guide Dog, and the Triumph of Trust at Ground Zero, by Michael Hingson and Susy Flory, follows Michael's story about growing up blind, his training in tech and his work with the Braille Literacy Campaign, and the training of his seeing-eye dogs. The play-by-play of how Michael and his guide dog made their way down so many flights of stairs—from a floor near Ray's—is gripping. When Elisa realized that was what her father's friend had actually experienced, it all truly sunk in.

Elisa and I talked, grownup to grownup, about that terrible day. We talked not only about the event itself, but how it had pulled our country together then. Patriotism helped people feel united, in our United States. But what a terrible way to have had to achieve that. I shared with her how hard I had tried to protect her innocence and had managed to do so for a short time. She can relate to that too, having toddler nieces she also wants to protect.

We talked, too, about how fascinating the training is for seeing-eye dogs. We'd shared an experience in Iowa, visiting a prison where they trained seeing-eye dogs. The Kiwanis Club, of which my husband was a member, was sponsoring a few dogs to help cover food, etc. Elisa remembered the testimony there of a blind man whose own guide dog had started training at that prison. The man had shared how his dog helped him navigate city streets, and said he once tried to step off a curb but his dog, seeing danger, refused to let him. On a note of humor, he also said his dog was trained to make a beeline for a coffee shop when told to "find Starbucks". A real live guide, vs. our now voice-activated GPS we ask to locate coffee for us.

It helped Elisa and me, reading about Michael, to truly visualize how a dog companion works, and to visualize how Michael's dog helped him navigate the many flights of stairs from the North Tower. It helped us imagine what that must have been like for Ray and to remember to pray for him, even today.

Protecting the innocence of our children—and now my grandchildren—is becoming increasingly difficult. Perhaps the trend to only recorded programming, such as Netflix, with a decrease in turning on live news, helps. But when we do have to share harsh realities with our children, it helps if we can also share hope: hope for a country united, and for the miraculous way even a dog can help save a human life.

— Laurie Winslow Sargent

THE IMPORTANCE OF MOURNING

There is a time for everything, and a season
for every activity under the heavens;
... a time to weep and a time to laugh,
a time to mourn and a time to dance
Ecclesiastes 3:1,4 (World English Bible)

I learned why grieving is important at the age of twenty-five, after the sudden death of my father. After I got "the call," I wanted to be strong for my mother. Somewhat mystified by my lack of tears, I went back to work only a few days after the funeral. Eighteen months later, frequent, unprovoked weeping helped me recognize the grip of clinical depression.

Fortunately, a path to grief counseling emerged – and I took it. Week after week, I sat in my counselor's office and poured my heart out. Starting with my recent loss, I went on to share the loss of other relatives, a disappointing relationship, and regrets about life choices. I realized I had figuratively stuffed my losses in a closet and shut the door, ignoring them until they poured out one day because the door was not strong enough to hold them all in. As I started to feel better, I knew the worst of my grieving was over.

Thankfully, I completed that mourning process and have applied the lessons many times since then. Years later, after my mother died, I warned my husband that if I felt like crying, I was going to cry. He did not fully understand until, years later, he lost his father.

Why do we mourn? To process grief and loss experienced by us, those we love, or even strangers. We do not have to know someone personally in order to relate to suffering. We recognize pain and we grieve with them.

Why do we need to mourn? To express ourselves in appropriate and meaningful ways, often connecting with others who share the same loss. Crying gives us a release of energy and pent-up negative feelings. Sharing experiences, especially common ones such as 9/11, provides healing because we are hard-wired for connection. Also, mourning can help us reflect on our own behaviors, and help us clearly view the actions, or inactions, of others; thereby providing insight.

Healthy mourning can be hard work. We want to believe in the old reality, and that life still goes on as it did before tragedy struck. Sharing memories and tears with close friends or family can be very helpful, as can spending time in prayer. Although the timeframe can differ by person, and some griefs come back to us at the oddest moments, deep mourning should come to a natural end. If not, we are fortunate to live in a time and place where assistance is available. Qualified, caring counselors help us work through our grief in a supportive setting. In conjunction with counseling, there are excellent, temporary pharmacological options when our brain chemistry becomes stuck in sadness. They can elevate our mood, moving us closer to our previous state.

Grief, and the way it is expressed, can be quite

different for different people. For large-scale grief, such as that created by the events of 9/11, specific times of remembrance allow us to give ourselves permission to grieve. Thus, we have 9/11, Memorial Day and Veteran's Day commemorations each year, available for the many who receive healing from the shared experience.

All of these options help us to regain our strength through mourning.

— Cynthia Baughan Wheaton

9/11 AND ME

It was a lovely, sunny Fall day. I woke early, showered, dressed and got ready to face the day. I made coffee, ate breakfast, prepared lunches for my daughter and husband, boiled my husband's breakfast egg and made his toast.

I drove my daughter to school and started my 30-minute commute to Jacksonville State University in Alabama where I taught English Composition, Literature and Speech. As always, I mentally went over my lesson plans for various classes during the drive.

Everything was as always. I greeted my colleagues and entered my office, stashing the books and papers I would need for class in a well-worn tote bag.

Suddenly, there was a commotion in the hallway outside my door, excited murmurings and one or two shouts. I ran to the door and spotted one of our teachers rushing toward me. Tears streamed down her face. I wasn't surprised. She was a very emotional person.

"Someone flew a plane into one of the World Trade Center Towers!"

Hearing that, I began to share a little of her distress. In 1945, I remembered, a B-25 bomber had accidentally flown into the Empire State Building during a heavy fog.

I'd recently read a book about the incident.

How terrible. It's happened again.

Not long after, as I walked along the hall to my first class, another faculty member announced to anybody who would listen that a second plane had crashed into the other tower at the World Trade Center!

These were not accidents!

My stomach twisted. I felt like I'd been struck in the face. Though my childhood in northern New York State was a long time ago and 1200 miles away, I was instantly a New Yorker again. Monstrous enemies were attacking my home state. And my country!

When I arrived in my classroom, I found everyone listening to the unfolding events on a portable radio. At the time, I occupied a very low place on the academic totem pole and was hesitant to cancel class.

"Please turn off the radio," I requested, trying not to notice the stricken faces of my students. In hindsight, I should have sat down and listened with them, or sent them all home, or something. I was trying to maintain normality, but these were events that would change the world, and merited attention.

I finished teaching my classes in a kind of daze, went home and planted myself in front of the television. What I saw was sickening.

The phone rang. It was my daughter's school, saying that an unidentified train had pulled into the local depot and the headmaster had decided to have the students "shelter in place." Our town was located next to a former military base, where tons of chemical weapons were being stored, awaiting destruction. Given the day's events, it was reasonable to fear that there might be an attack on the base.

I knew one thing: if my daughter was in any kind of

danger, her place was with me, not at school. I would go get her, and they were welcome to try and stop me!

Just as I was about to leave, there was another phone call. My elder brother Andrew was somewhere in Manhattan and couldn't be reached. I knew he had occasionally worked in the World Trade Center and knew many people there.

Would he join the first responders and run into the building? That would be like him! Or what if he had been in the office of one of those friends when the planes hit?

I wouldn't allow myself to think about that, but I could pray, and I did, with all my heart!

As I drove, I pictured my beautiful, bright, blue-eyed daughter Ellen, the girl with the ready smile who owned at least half of my heart. And there was my big brother, who had looked after me when I fell on the playground, trying to cheer me up as I cried. He'd taught me how to throw a softball, how to care for my turtles, how to tell time and a host of other life skills. It had been my brother's wife who'd called to tell me she couldn't locate him. They had two children. What would their lives be like without him?

At the school, I walked briskly into the headmaster's office and blurted, "I want to take my daughter home. I'm from New York and my brother's missing in Manhattan." And then burst into tears.

The headmaster Mr. Gorey was kindness itself. Walking around his big desk, he gave me a hug and immediately summoned my daughter. Ellen was fifteen, clearly old enough to understand what was happening. We drove back in companionable silence and watched TV until my husband Tom came home, bringing with him a sense of calm. Then, dinner and more TV.

At last, the call came: my brother was found! As an attorney for the state university, he had been attending a meeting with other lawyers in the midtown School of Optometry and had a clear view of the catastrophe. After seeing the towers fall, he and his colleagues, some of whom were nurses, immediately adjourned the meeting and headed downtown to see what they could do to help.

The Red Cross blood bank was already swamped with donors, so they dropped the nurses off at first aid stations and joined the hundreds of thousands of New Yorkers heading north on foot, in compliance with Mayor Guiliani's directions. Later, Andrew was able to find a train going upstate and was grateful to sit on the floor all the way to Poughkeepsie and then catch a ride with another university employee back to Albany. Finally, late that night, disheveled and exhausted but thankful, he arrived home.

We were also relieved to learn that the train in Anniston that had caused such concern proved to be no threat, but saddened that a lady in our community lost her son at the Pentagon.

That sunny September day changed my life, changed all our lives. We could never again take for granted our peaceful happy lives.

Terror was real, and it had entered our country!

— *Louise Sowa*

PERSPECTIVE

The knock at the door was a welcomed sound. Finally, the school maintenance man had come to repair the refrigerator. We were living in a little house provided by my husband's alma mater where he was teaching and coaching the men's basketball team. After many years, he found himself back in this small Mississippi town. There were challenges in our 875-square-foot, free accommodations on the edge of the school bus parking lot. Most of our worldly possessions had been stored in a spare classroom in the gym. With three teenage boys and a young daughter, we were cramped in the furnished three-bedroom dwelling. The shower had been remodeled for a previous tenant who must have been short, because the shower head sprayed my shoulder and every time I washed my hair, my hands hit the ceiling. In the corner, I could see the ground through a hole in the bathroom linoleum.

I opened the door to greet the man who had come to my rescue. His face said, "What is it this time?" This handy man had been called on frequently to repair the floor furnace so it would work, to spray for roaches so I didn't have to use a fly swatter in one hand and a spatula in the other while making pancakes, and to put a doorknob with a lock on our bedroom door.

His face paled and I knew there was more on his mind. Then he spoke, "Morning...did you hear what happened?" I could tell right away it was something shocking. "My son is in the military, he got word that a plane crashed into the North Twin Tower this morning and about 15 minutes later another plane crashed into the South Tower. Turn on the news."

I ran to the television and turned to one of the three channels our antenna received. There it was. Over and over, they played the videos of the planes crashing into the towers. For days, I sat in the wooden rocking chair, mesmerized by the news. I had a trip planned to Brazil at the end of October for the birth of my first grandchild. I wondered if the flight would actually happen. Airports had been closed everywhere. Would they be open in six weeks? As I rocked and listened, I was crocheting a baby blanket for the coming newborn, working my yarn, stitch after stitch, in tandem with the rhythm of my rocks. The baby blanket was growing to cover a king-sized bed. I felt like I was doing something constructive to fix the world.

I had the typical questions: "How could this happen? Where was God in this?" So many people died. Then, I began hearing the stories of people God protected. I heard about the whole office of people who had worked on a project late into the night and planned to come in after lunch. Someone told me about the subway pay-ment system that malfunctioned and people couldn't buy rides to get to work in the towers. Another story cir-culated about the person who overslept. She was ironing by the window and looked up just in time to see her office destroyed. If her alarm had gone off as usual, she would have been in the building.

In the big picture of these current events, my complaints about the home God provided seemed so minor, so insignificant. I had no threat of death. I had so many reasons to be grateful. I had an indoor shower with hot running water and clean hair. I was fully alive. My children were safe. God is still in place. Trust. Hope. Perspective.

— Dea Irby

OVERCOME

The walls of my cubicle were thin that day
With the woman beside me laughing
About a plane
That struck a building
In New York City.

My questions flooded the air between us.
Was it a prop plane?
How was the pilot?
Was anyone hurt?
She did not answer.
I was new and friendless in that job
And I couldn't find my footing.

Then another plane struck
And a television said D.C. was burning.
So I broke the rules to call my mother
Who said Dad was in New York.
The walls of the cubicle grew thicker
And closed in around me like an iron vise.
Before the day was out,
Our parking garage was burning too.
A coincidence, they said.
It felt like the end of the world.

Meanwhile…

My father stood for ages in the bowels of the subway

Looking into the dark for a train that was late.
He was frustrated and annoyed
On this regular day
On his regular way
To a meeting in a room high above the sidewalks.

When the subway cars arrived
They were packed
With riders and panicked faces.
My father watched a homeless woman
Embrace a well-dressed stranger.
They cried together,
Sharing the moment
And what looked like fear.

It was baffling
And unsettling
For those like my father
Who knew nothing of the mayhem
And the destruction
Above them.

Their sheltered oblivion wouldn't last,
But the bafflement
Would soon multiply.

My father emerged from the tunnels
To a chorus of sirens.
As a firetruck tilted into a turn,
The fireman standing on the back
Stared at my father and my father back at him
For one eternal moment,
Transmitting a terrified urgency.

Through this brief connection,
An electric energy,
Raw and gritty,
Flowed unbridled from one man to the other.

My father went upstairs for his meeting
At a school of optometry
Where vision is refined, healed and preserved.
As he stood by a window

Watching the chaos of the people and the cars and the
firetrucks in the streets,
He saw the second plane hit
And then each tower collapse.

He encouraged students to go wash building dust
and ashes
From people's eyes.
He helped find stranded people a way out of the city
Or a place to stay.
He escorted some on an hours-long trip
Toward the warm, grounded shelter of our home.
He was alive
He was grateful.
I imagine he's scarred.

For days, we heard stories of friends who lost friends,
Acquaintances who lost family,
Rumors of phone calls answered and missed,
And final I love yous.
We shared pain as we binged on TV reports
And tearful musical tributes.

My Gran ached to help,
And packed her bags for a trip
All the way from Alabama
To feed workers on the ground.

She has a cough sometimes, even still,
And a hard hat, I think,
And memories of a kind man adorned
In thousands of safety pins
Who led her from a bad neighborhood
To a good one,
To her cramped room at the Y.

Today, I am a million years removed from that job.

I am no longer
Crushed between those cubicle walls.
The world did not end,
And my father came home to us.

Still... the ghosts of that day remain.
Sometimes, when the sun shines brightly
And the air is crisp and still,
I am overcome all over again
By the falling ash,
The falling people,
My father's resolve,
My grandmother's heart,
That fireman's electrified bravery,
New York City's stubborn will,
And the never-ending blue sky
Of that beautiful, broken day.

— *Kate Edwards Trussler*

A TUESDAY MORNING TO REMEMBER

On a brisk Tuesday morning in September in the early part of this century, I had just left my warm bed and begun to get ready to go to my job at Carbite Golf in San Diego, California when my phone rang. It was my husband calling. He managed a small restaurant and had left home earlier to get ready for his breakfast customers.

"Turn on the TV," he said. "A plane just hit one of the Twin Towers in New York. Some idiot flew too low and crashed into it."

I turned on the set and to my surprise saw another plane fly into the second tower. "That's no accident," we said in unison. "Those planes hit the towers on purpose!"

I stood transfixed to the screen, not believing what I was seeing. Plumes of smoke rose from the windows far up in the buildings. The announcers tried to make sense of the unbelievable scenario unfolding before them. People covered in ash ran screaming in all directions. The cameras veered away from the windows when it was announced that people were jumping from the upper stories to escape the fire. Such a sight was too horrific to witness.

I had to get ready for work but was so mesmerized I couldn't leave the room. Then, right before my eyes, the second tower began to collapse, sinking down, down, down, until there was nothing left but a mountainous pile of steel and ash. I couldn't speak, it was all too unbelievable. I was three thousand miles away, but felt as though I were an eye witness to the tragedy.

As the world stood in awe, it was reported that another plane had slammed into the Pentagon followed shortly thereafter by a plane crash in a field in Pennsylvania. Thanks to the selfless efforts of the passengers, who took on the hijackers and managed to keep the plane from hitting the Capitol Building, the presumed target. It was now clear that this was a planned attack on the United States, leaving us with no idea how many more planes would be involved.

In a daze, I went to work and managed to get through the day, feeling a kindred spirit to my parents' generation and how they must have felt after the attack on Pearl Harbor. It was clear that life changed after both events and would never be the same again.

On Wednesday at noon, I watched as all of Congress stood on the steps of the Capitol and sang "God Bless America." No Republicans, no Democrats, just Americans, every one of them in solid unity. The song sent shivers down my back as I heard, really heard, the words to the song. I was never so proud to be an American as at that moment. Seeing our country's leaders come together with no thought of politics was a special moment, even if it didn't last past a day or two.

For the next few days, nearly every car sported a flag and did what they could to show allegiance to this country and to show the foreign invaders that they didn't win.

On Friday, a Carbite salesman asked if I wanted to attend a church memorial service during our lunch hour.

Four of us attended the service and prayed hard for our country and for the nearly three thousand who lost their lives in the unprecedented terrorist attack.

Later, I learned that my girlfriend in Tennessee who had decided to get back into the work force, had signed up to be a flight attendant with Southwest Airlines. After doing all the home study work, she finally was told to appear at the Southwest terminal to start her on-the-job training. She walked in and saw people milling around the raised television sets and assumed it was all part of her training. Her first day on the job was the morning of September 11, 2001. She soon learned that it was no training film, she was watching the Twin Towers going down. A very inglorious and scary introduction to the job of flight attendant.

All of us have been affected by this horrible event in one way or another. Life, and our freedom, has changed in a way we never could have imagined.

— Linda Loegel

WHAT IS YOUR EMERGENCY?

Our minds are funny things, always playing tricks on us. When you see the number 911 most of us probably think, EMERGENCY. But when those same numbers are written 9/11, most of us, especially those who are old enough to remember, think of 9/11/2001. The reality, 9/11 was one of the most, if not the most, horrifying emergencies our nation has faced in decades. On a clear Tuesday morning, a well-planned attack by was carried out by 19 militants associated with the Islamic extremist group al-Qaeda. It was the deadliest attack on American soil in United States history.

I was home schooling my three children at the time. At 8:30 am that morning we pulled into a church parking lot to register for CO-OP classes. A few short minutes later, we gathered in prayer, praying for our nation, before heading back home to watch the day's events unfold. I remember my children studying my reaction.

I first called my cousin who lived in New Jersey. Her husband traveled frequently and I wanted to know if he was okay. I spoke with my brother to share our grief. My husband arrived back home from a meeting. The five of us watched our small television in the upstairs playroom of our new home in North Carolina. We cried, we prayed. For the next several days, weeks, the news was filled with 9/11. That day will never be the same for so many Americans, those who were personally affected and those of us who remember. But today, two decades later, while certain things remain etched in my memory, my reflections are not the same. My thoughts are bit broader, my grief a bit deeper.

Over the years there have been several conspiracy theories that surround 9/11. Who was really behind this heinous act? Was it a foreign government, an extremist group whose goal is to destroy Christians? Those are the questions I have when I think of 9/11.

That date forces me to ponder a new emergency. The emergency of sin. That tiny three-letter word that affects all of us. That tiny three-letter word that, if left unchecked, leads us to more sin. That tiny three-letter word that if we do not recognize, if we do not bring it to the foot of the cross, leads us to further and maybe permanent separation from God.

Why is it so hard for us to talk about sin? None of us is exempt. We all fall short, every day. We all miss the mark. It is a reality that we cannot escape. Evil does exist. There is evil in our world, and evil in our hearts. Unfortunately, I think most of us would be surprised if we knew just how evil, evil is. It roams the earth seeking those whom it can devour. Our enemy never relents, he never sleeps, and when confronted, fights harder.

BUT GOD. While there is an emergency called sin, God is our 911. Only God can defeat sin. Jesus Christ is the solution to our evil. Holy Spirit, the helper we need to live victoriously over the spirit of darkness. And while evil can lead to many destructive things, there is one thing evil will never do. Evil will never win. It was defeated 2,000 years ago. And if we learn how to fight it, we can continue to defeat it in our hearts, in our country and in our world.

— Karyn Mulligan

WHAT A DIFFERENCE A DAY MAKES

I was getting ready to go to work and was in the kitchen eating the last of my breakfast. It was a gorgeous September day in north central Pennsylvania, with clear blue skies, brilliant sunshine, and leaves at the tops of the nearby mountains just starting to turn yellow and orange. The television was on and regular programming was interrupted by a news bulletin to say that at 8:46 AM an airplane had crashed into the North Tower of the World Trade Center in New York City. My heart skipped a beat.

The telephone rang twice in succession. I answered twice to first speak to our daughter and then our son who both asked the same question, "Where's Dad?"

"In New York City."

"Have you heard from him?"

My answer was the same each time. "No, but I'm going to call Phyllis next. As soon as I hear anything I'll call you."

Upon disconnecting from the kids, I dialed the phone to call George's assistant. My eyes were glued to the television screen as the phone was ringing at Woolrich, Inc.

Riveted in front of the breaking news, I was no

longer interested in breakfast or work. I watched and listened as the reporters speculated as to why a plane would or could hit such a prominent building in lower Manhattan. My husband was in the city on one of his routine business trips. Phyllis answered. I told her what happened. George's staff in Woolrich turned their television set on in the break room. Phyllis assured me that when she reached him, she'd have him call me.

Minutes later, George was on the phone. Phyllis had told him what happened. Although he was in Manhattan, news from the lower part of the city hadn't yet reached him. While we were still talking, at 9:03 AM, I watched as the cameras trained on the buildings captured a second aircraft as it flew into the South Tower. All major networks covered the incident and, by this time, everyone knew it was deliberate. I cried out, "George, New York is under attack. You have to get out. Get the car and, please, leave now."

"Nance, I can't. I'm standing here in the lobby of the hotel. We're getting reports from an officer at the desk that all the bridges and tunnels are being closed. I couldn't leave if I wanted to."

"Did you check out already? Rooms are going to be scarce."

"I did, but they're assuring me a place to stay tonight."

"What are you going to do now?" I asked.

"I'm going to keep what client appointments I can and go to the credit group meeting we have scheduled this afternoon. I'm not sure how many people will show up under the circumstances. I've got to stay busy or this will drive me crazy."

"If you can, call me later. I've heard on the news that all the cell towers are shut down."

"I will. Yes, all cell towers are down. The desk clerk

tells me that they'll inform guests as soon as the NYPD has opened up an exit route. Right now only emergency vehicles are getting into the city. I have to go so someone else can use the phone. Love you, bye."

I had immense relief that he was safe and even more relief that the hotel made sure he wouldn't be spending the night on the street. I guessed that being a client of thirty years has its perks. However, I had an ominous feeling that the attacks were just beginning.

I faced both the TV screen and the window looking out over the valley through which the West Branch of the Susquehanna River flowed. It was eerily serene considering what was happening to the east of us in New York City.

Around 9:10 AM, immediately after I got off the phone with George, I saw an unusual sight. A large passenger plane passed over our valley heading west. I thought it odd because, although we were in the flight pattern, planes were usually at a much higher altitude. I glanced back at the TV set broadcasting news bulletins from New York City and reports of aircraft all over the nation being grounded. I looked back at the plane flying over our valley getting smaller in the distance. I had a strange sense of foreboding. Was it my overactive imagination?

At 9:37 AM, hijackers aboard American Airlines Flight 77 crashed into the western side of the Pentagon in Washington, D.C. killing fifty-nine aboard the plane and one hundred twenty-five military and civilian personnel inside the building. Three attacks on our nation in less than an hour. We were definitely under siege. How many more people were going to die today?

The South Tower of the World Trade Center collapsed at 9:59 AM. TV cameras caught it all. Evacuees, on-lookers, and reporters ran for their lives. People flee-ing the site were covered from head to toe in grey ash. I thought of our friends who worked in those buildings. Were they safe?

The media began to report conversations heard by Air Traffic Controllers from the cockpit of one of the hijacked planes. Family members at home were talking to loved ones on the aircraft with messages of love and final goodbyes. Passengers told family members they were attempting to take back United Airlines Flight 93 in the air over Pennsylvania. In an emotional conversa-tion with his wife, Todd Beamer uttered those famous words to his fellow heroes, "Let's roll!" In response to the resistance, the hijackers deliberately crashed the plane into a field in Shanksville, Pennsylvania shortly after 10 AM, killing all aboard. Investigators learned that Flight 93's original mission was to crash into the Capitol Building in Washington, D.C.

I couldn't stay at home alone to think about every-thing happening and my husband being stuck in the city, so I went to work for a few hours. The office was sub-dued. Patients were calling to cancel their appointments, stating they were too upset to come in. Everyone seemed to be moving robotically just trying to get through the day. As soon as I got home, I emailed my friend Jay who worked at the World Trade Center. "Please contact me. I'm worried about you," I typed. I awaited word from family members of others we knew.

After a fitful night's sleep, I answered the phone at 8 AM when George called, saying the NYPD had opened one lane of the George Washington Bridge for traffic leaving the city. He would be home in about four hours. I offered up a prayer of thanksgiving and began to plan a meal of comfort foods. We were going to need comfort.

On September 12, 2001, American flags were flying from every house and business in Lock Haven, Pennsylvania. The national news showed the same phenomenon from coast to coast. The nation was united in shock, grief, and mourning. Citizens pulled together and stood shoulder to shoulder with a profound sense of patriotism.

In later days, the nation got details of Firefighters, EMTs, Law Enforcement Officers, and ordinary citizens who did extraordinary things to save lives that day. The passengers who valiantly fought hijackers for control of Flight 93 were among these heroes.

Epilogue

On September 14, our son called to say that there was no news from his friend Martin who worked for Cantor Fitzgerald in the North Tower. The family was hoping that he had survived but the odds were not in his favor. The reporters had begun interviewing survivors and family members who had spoken to their loved ones inside the burning buildings. Cantor Fitzgerald could not account for six hundred fifty-eight of their nine hundred sixty workers occupying floors 101 through 105. When American Airlines Flight 11 flew into floors 93 through 99 of the North Tower, the Boeing 767 was traveling at four hundred seventy miles per hour. The craft measured one hundred fifty-six feet from wingtip to wingtip and carried 10,000 gallons of jet fuel. After the initial impact, a shock wave radiated up and down the building, shaking the huge structure. We prayed for a miracle that Martin would be found safe.

Three days later, I received an email from my friend, Jay. He recounted that he watched as the second plane hit the South Tower. His building was evacuated and everyone ran for their lives as the buildings collapsed and spewed thick gray ash over all of lower Manhattan. He walked for hours, eventually crossing the George Washington Bridge on foot along with hundreds of others. Once on the Jersey side, he called for someone to pick him up and take him home. Thank God, he was spared.

Hearing that my friend Amy was safe at home after the attacks on New York City was another huge relief. Amy was eight months pregnant. She and her husband were eagerly looking forward to being first-time parents. She worked at American Express across the street from the World Trade Center in a job she loved in the city she loved.

On the morning of 9/11, Amy was thinking about her 9 AM meeting as she crossed over the West Side Highway via the pedestrian bridge. She was startled by a loud roaring noise and began to see white papers falling from the sky. Everyone began to run, including eight-month-pregnant Amy. She made it across the bridge into the atrium and joined up with a friend. Grabbing Megan's hand tightly, Amy took charge and led her through the streets to the water's edge a few blocks away where they could clearly see black billowing smoke pouring from the North Tower. They were told that an airplane had hit the building.

At that moment, the growing crowd at the dock seeking to escape the inferno heard another low-flying jumbo jet. They watched in horror as it banked and plowed into the South Tower, spewing fuel and flames throughout the damaged floors. It was then everyone knew New York City was under attack.

Amy and Megan found seats on a crowded ferry. Amy insisted that the crew give her a life jacket. She told me that all she could think of was Pearl Harbor. She was convinced that the ferry boats would be attacked next. If she was wearing a life jacket, she reasoned, at least she would float enabling someone to save her and her unborn child.

The two young women had no idea where this ferry would dock, they just knew they had to get away from the carnage. When the boat pulled into a berth at Hoboken, it discharged hundreds of passengers and returned to the New York side to retrieve more. The two women found their way to the New Jersey Transit and boarded a train heading west. As they rode in silence, the women checked for cell service. As soon as they could, they called their frantic family members to meet them at the station. Amy related to me that it was a tearful, joyous reunion but, that night, she could not begin to close her eyes. The aftermath of an intense survival mode adrenaline rush had worn off and anxiety had set in. She had to turn on every light in the house to feel safe enough to sleep.

One month later, Amy delivered a healthy baby boy. It was almost a year before she went back to work in the city. Everything had changed. Not one employee could sit on the side of the office to look out the windows facing east. Where the once majestic World Trade Center Towers stood was a deep, dark pit in the earth. Many people in the office found themselves breaking into tears from the mere proximity of what remained as a result of evil perpetrated upon our nation that glorious fall day in September. Workers still combed through the debris looking for evidence of those unaccounted for.

One day, I got a call from my son that Martin's wedding ring had been found in the pile. His wife identified it from the inscription inside. Martin's family finally had closure.

After reading the National Transportation Safety Board report some years later, my husband and I determined that Flight 93 had been the aircraft I saw flying above the West Branch of the Susquehanna. It was not my imagination. This nation had gone from living in freedom one day to living in fear the next. The United States of America was forever changed.

— *Nancy Panko*

THE AFTERMATH

September 11, 2002: Grandson Jacob
was eighteen months old and the power of the hatred
on that day, one year ago, still haunted me.
I wrote this poem for him.

The Aftermath

September 11, 2002
9-11 used to be an ordinary day.
Now it's time for people to gather and pray!
On this September 11, it's been one entire year,
Since the all world has known such terrible fear.

Terrorists' actions united Americans to be strong,
Together we work trying to undo any wrong.
We mourn our losses and Americans now demonstrate
Strong patriotism and strength giving us
reasons to celebrate.

Red, white and blue adorn lapels across our nation,
The waving of flags brings hope
for our future generation.
Ordinary people became heroes that day
So other families could be safe in every way.

Our spirits bloomed and our hopes are high,
We fight against the terrible things
that happened in the sky.
We won't let Bin Laden show us defeat.
American will triumph making terrorism obsolete.

— *Terry Hans*

SEPTEMBER MOURNING

The first time I saw the World Trade Center Twin Towers, they were brand new. They stood gleaming; golden orange as the sun reflected off them. I marveled at the masterpieces of architecture which were in the center of the Commerce District. They held thousands of workers and their children who were in daycare facilities This was my first trip to New York City.

The next time I went to the city was May of 2002. There was a vast hole full of debris. The fence which surrounded the area held fliers containing descriptions and photos of missing persons. I couldn't help but think they were left there so long because the person that posted it knew their brother, father, son, daughter or spouse was already dead, or possibly buried under the mass of twisted metal, concrete and ash.

The starkness of it all hit me and I began to cry. I took my husband's hand and we made our way toward the subway. We were on our honeymoon. I wonder how many newlyweds were ripped apart that beautiful, clear fall day.

Like so many others that day, I remember what I was doing when I first heard the news. I was driving on Route 33 between Massanutten and Stanardsville,

Virginia, where I was living at the time. I turned the radio on a music station and heard that one of the Twin Towers had been hit by an airplane. I thought it had to be a commercial, perhaps a movie trailer, and changed the station. Next, I heard the South Tower had collapsed and I felt like I had been hit in the stomach by one of the medicine balls we used to toss around in gym class. This was for real.

I wasn't in shock. I was more in a trance-like state. I was able to keep driving but kept looking into other cars to see if I could tell by the driver's faces whether or not they had heard the news. When I reached home, I immediately turned on the television and watched the horror, transfixed on the surreal videos until I couldn't stand it anymore. Wearily, I went to my room, crawled into bed and hoped it would all turn out just to be a nightmare, I fell asleep.

I awoke to find the nightmare continuing. My emotions were like leaves blowing around in the fall. First, there was a little good news, like someone was found in the rubble and it lightened my mood a little.

Then the media played the calls of people frantic to reach loved ones to try to find them or to say goodbye to the ones they knew could never reach safety. It was mind-numbing and it hurt my heart as well.

My mood plummeted close to the ground, only to waft upward when it turned out someone whose family members thought they were dead had turned up.

I remember the bravest of the brave first responders, who lost their lives helping others come down from the towers, then those who worked amidst all the rubble and heaps of hot metal exhausted from looking for survivors. Many of them would be diagnosed with lung disease or lung cancer from the soot and filth they travailed in day after day. There are many good things to remember, but many others we want to forget.

The most outstanding things I remember are how this tragedy bound this country together. Everyone forgot their differences. American flags hung from almost every edifice. "We'll never forget" t-shirts were everywhere. People sang "God Bless America" with gusto. Strangers helped and hugged each other, rejoiced and mourned together.

People looked up with respect to the mayor of New York and the President of the United states. We treated first responders like the heroes they were and are.

Here we are, twenty years later. I have to ask, "Have we forgotten?" A nation, once united, is now divided. Instead of policemen being seen as the heroes they are, they are assaulted. Police cars are burned and turned over. They have been expelled from restaurants. Two were ambushed and while fighting for their lives in the hospital, people outside were chanting that they hoped they would die.

These days, God is left out of almost everything. We prayed a lot during those days, but now prayer is censored, for the most part. Respect has not been shown for the office of the President. Instead of pulling together, people are tearing cities apart, rioting, looting, and burning the businesses of hard working citizens to the ground. We all cried after 9/11, but shouldn't we be crying now? What will it take to bring this country together again? I shudder to think what it might be.

— ***Maribeth Hynnes Stevens***

SO FAR, YET SO NEAR

Disrupted

My husband's feet thundered down the two flights of stairs from his third-floor office. What was that all about? Ever since working together as consultants in our North Carolina home, I had come to recognize that sound. Something big had happened. Loud, fast foot-steps meant Jim was bringing news – either really good or very bad. Did we get a new client? Had someone died?

Earlier, our two children had climbed onto the school bus in front of our home, anticipating another ordinary elementary school day. After turning off the morning news at around 8:40 am, I was in my first-floor office, just over an hour into working on time-sensitive dead-lines. The usual morning rush was over and a normal Tuesday morning was in process.

At the sound of Jim's feet, I was more curious than annoyed about the impending interruption.

"What's going on?" I called out as, surprisingly, he ran past my office at the bottom of the stairs and headed to the kitchen. He did not even look my way as he called out, "Two planes have hit the World Trade Center!"

Immediately, we both knew one crash could be an accident. But, two? What was happening?

I rushed to join him in front of our 14-inch television on the kitchen counter. As it flickered on, our first view was of a split screen, both sides showing close-ups of burning buildings. The left side was labeled "Washington, D.C.," and the right side "New York." Our minds raced to catch up as we tried to focus.

My Life Intertwined with Washington

Based on the news bulletin Jim had received, we were expecting to see the World Trade Center Towers in New York City. But, D.C.? My thoughts immediately moved to my sister and her family. They had lived in our nation's Capital for over thirty years. My brother-in-law worked very close to the White House. They lived a mere dozen blocks from the U.S. Capitol building. Fortunately, I was fairly certain that their two sons were on distant college campuses.

I had visited the area many times and had lasting, wonderful memories. Every few years during my childhood, my parents took us there to visit the Smithsonian museum, the National Gallery, the Washington Monument, and more. On July 4, 1976, our country's Bi-Centennial, I listened, along with my sister and her husband, to a powerful reading of the Declaration of Independence from the steps of the National Archives. Next, we had gone to the Capitol building, where punch and cookies were served to the public, along with an open tour of both chambers. In 1988, my husband and I spent time there on our honeymoon, soaking in the Air and Space Museum before a wonderful family dinner. I knew this area and people I loved were there!

My second, almost immediate thought, was tied to childhood nightmares. I was raised in Richmond, Virginia during the Cold War, only one hundred miles from Washington. Speculation about nuclear attacks on Washington took place on an ongoing basis. Civil defense drills occurred often in my schools. Evacuation routes were published on the front page of the local newspaper, and made quite an impression on my young mind. I also remember my father's calm and practical voice as he explained them.

My father, a co-owner of a concrete products business, had developed prototypes of bomb shelters in 1961. At the age of seven, I would go with my parents and older sister to visit bomb shelters installed in the backyards of local homes. They often were damp, and always small. Generally, they had been installed by European survivors of World War II's devastation. Most were stocked with canned goods, water and the basics of life.

My concerns as a seven-year-old were how our family of four would fit in the claustrophobic space, and how we could store the clothes that would accommodate our growing bodies throughout the two years that we would need to remain inside. There was a profound moment when my mother explained that our dog would not be allowed to join us. Although we never discussed it at the time, my sister and I later talked about the terror we felt.

My father worked with Virginia officials to create a bomb shelter to display at the 1961 Virginia State Fair. A local disc jockey agreed to live inside this above-ground sample shelter for the duration of the ten-day fair. There was a large window on the side, with curtains he could open when he was broadcasting, allowing people to see and talk to him.

After the fair, my father stopped focusing on bomb shelters. We never installed one in our yard, and his company never offered them for sale. I believe my parents decided to rely on their deep faith that God would be with us, regardless of the circumstances, rather than cling to the strategy of a desperate, bleak, below-ground attempt at survival.

Washington Reality

Suddenly, the current situation came into focus. The Pentagon had been hit in addition to the World Trade Center Towers. Beyond comprehension! I often had driven across the Potomac River on the 14th Street Bridge, from Virginia into D.C., as planes took off from National Airport (now Reagan International) just above my head. The Pentagon, although only five stories high, is a massive structure. It is near the highway, on the left, as the low Washington skyline comes into view. I vividly could visualize the crash.

I was reasonably certain that I knew no one at the Pentagon, and felt somewhat guilty at my immediate relief. Nevertheless, a number of people, and probably many, had instantly perished. How awful for those on the plane, who knew they were flying far too low and clearly in an ominous direction!

My family-related relief was short-lived. We soon heard about another plane, possibly heading to Washington, with dozens of people – still alive – on board. What was the plane's target? I thought again of my extended family. They must still be in potential danger, and rushing to figure out their next steps.

We, along with many, many panicked people, were discovering that phone connections, both mobile and land-line, were overwhelmed in the two cities under attack; and, indeed, across the entire country. Just about everyone was reaching out, wanting to touch base with the people they cared about most, even if they were not in harm's way. We all wanted to connect. There was nothing else we could do but watch – and pray.

My Life Intertwined with New York

Jim's and my attention turned back to New York, a city we both knew well. Jim had lived in the metropolitan area for much of his life, and worked in mid-town Manhattan early in his business career. I had traveled there regularly on business for almost a decade. The towers we had seen many times were burning, and it was clear that a lot of innocent people were trapped. Could those above the crash areas make it to the roof? Why was no one up there? Helicopters were circling, but dense smoke made visibility difficult.

What about people in the Windows on the World restaurant, located on the top floors of Tower One? In 2000, it had been the highest grossing restaurant in the United States, with $37 million in sales. Located on floors 106 and 107, the views were remarkable. Locals and visitors alike considered it a must-experience restaurant.

In the 1980s, an advertising agency I was working with took me to Windows on the World as a special treat. After the ear-popping ascent, requiring two different elevators, they insisted that I take a choice seat next to the huge glass windows. The Manhattan-area view was gorgeous, and we could see clearly for miles.

I quickly pulled back, because the window next to me revealed an unbelievable drop. We were so high that the ground below was difficult to even see. I became dizzy as I peered down from the offered seat. I refused to sit there!

The restaurant staff told us that the towers were designed to sway in the wind, somewhat similar to the flexibility built into high-rise structures near California's fault lines. Considering the one-acre size of each floor, this flexibility was astounding to consider. In fact, we felt it slowly sway a bit during dinner. And, it was not even particularly windy outside. I did not like the feeling at all! I had no interest in lingering over dinner and, after the stomach-churning ride down, was happy to return to solid ground.

My husband and I were familiar with another aspect of the Twin Towers. In 1986, we traveled to New York to make a presentation to clients at American Express. Because their office was at 200 Vesey Street, across from the seven-building World Trade Center (WTC), we took a subway from our hotel and got off at the Tower Station, which was buried deep below street level. We rode up a several-stories-tall escalator, pressed together with a mass of people who were starting their day. As we scurried through the dramatic, high-ceilinged lobby, many commuters headed for the elevators within the building. We exited, walked across the courtyard, then crossed West Street to our destination. Wind whipped around us, as is common near skyscrapers. After our meeting, we retraced our steps through the complex, and headed north on the subway to mid-town Manhattan's Grand Central Station.

In March 1998, my husband stayed at the Marriott Hotel at WTC 3, while on a business trip. The shortest building at the World Trade Center, nestled between Tower One and Tower Two, was ideal for anyone with meetings in the complex.

Throughout my years of New York business travel, I worked with many people who lived in the metro area. I was not close to many, but I cared about them all. Where were they and their families? Were they safe? Did I know anyone who had traveled there for business?

New York Reality

The horror faced by the desperate people standing in the open windows on the high floors of the World Trade Center was acutely vivid to me. I knew from experience how tiny the cars and people were below. What would I do? Which of the horrific options would I choose? I could not imagine having so little time to make such a ghastly decision.

As I watched, I knew that if I were trying to make my way out of the building, or clinging to an empty window frame, I would be praying. I also knew that many watching on television were asking for God's mercy on those in danger. God was in those places of shock, fear and desperation.

Oddly, the buildings looked as if they were starting to bulge in the middle. Could that be an optical illusion? Was it possible the buildings would collapse? Had they stopped subway trains from entering the station beneath the buildings? And, what of the rescue personnel pouring into the area? So many questions as the minutes ticked onward!

During our watching and waiting, still huddled in front of the small kitchen television, I called a neighbor. Our daughters were best friends, and I knew her husband was out of town on business. This would be a terrible thing to experience alone. We did not have to persuade her to join us. She quickly drove down, and planned to stay until her kids, and ours, arrived on the bus. We finally moved to the much-larger television in the family room. We continued to watch the horrible events as they were unfolding, often switching channels, mesmerized.

Just before 10 am, the South Tower, WTC 2, suddenly collapsed, spewing a dense white, exploding fog of detritus into the surrounding streets. The collapse was eerily silent to us, as we watched it through the long-distance lenses of television cameras. The sound must have been horrendous, especially to those inside. We were incredulous at what we were witnessing.

Mere minutes later, there was news that a plane had crashed into a field near Shanksville, Pennsylvania. All other planes within the entire U.S. airspace had been grounded. Therefore, this almost certainly was the final plane that had turned off its communication devices, and deviated from its flight plan. We rejoiced that there were no more immediate threats from rogue planes. At the same time, we mourned the additional loss of innocent lives.

Jim and I had always tried to keep our family, and especially our parents, informed of our physical location during any emergency. Years of business travel had instilled this habit into us. That day, we knew Jim's parents were planning to travel from Connecticut to visit Jim's mother's parents in New Hampshire. At 10:10 am, my husband sent his parents the following email: "In case you're in New Hampshire and have figured out how to check your emails when you're away… neither Cynthia nor I were traveling to [our client] in New York today, and we don't believe we know anyone who works in the World Trade Center."

Eighteen minutes later, more tragedy. Suddenly but not unexpectedly, the North Tower, WTC 1, collapsed. As the building disintegrated, our sense of urgency was transformed into despair. How could anyone survive that?

My husband and I are analytical people by nature and profession. It might sound ghoulish to some, but we started linearly and probabilistically estimating the number of people in the World Trade Center who had perished. My estimate – which I hoped was incorrect – was 10,000. Jim's estimate of no more than 5,000 turned out to be much closer to the actual number of 2,763. Nonetheless, far too many were lost.

Also, as did most people, we realized early on that the date of 9/11 was eerily similar to the well-known 9-1-1 emergency phone number. Could this have been part of the perpetrators' plan? If not, it was an incredible coincidence. So many questions!

Seeking Normalcy

Jim went back up to his office just after 1 pm. Focusing on his emails would be a calming distraction. He replied to one from an industry contact, written on September 10th, requesting a conference call on the 11th. Jim replied: "Thank you for your email. Yes, let's talk… however, not today. Cynthia and I have been watching the devastation in New York and DC, including the live collapse of the second WTC Tower, and it's very upsetting." Upsetting, to say the least.

Around 2:50 p.m., we went out to the bus stop, to meet our kids. We weren't sure what they knew, because there had been so little contact from their school. We never should have doubted that they would have known about the tragedy! Our third-grader's teacher had informed his class of the basics, in age-appropriate language. Sadly, we learned that our fifth-grader's teacher had tuned the classroom television to the one channel that had included coverage of victims falling to their deaths. A terrible thing for anyone to watch! But, particularly horrific for youngsters.

After our two children walked into the house, they ran immediately to the playroom, which did not contain a television. They needed time to process what had happened, without additional input.

Our home phone rang, and I was surprised to hear my mother-in-law's voice. After expressing my joy at hearing from her, she was puzzled. How did I know to be worried about them? It turned out that they knew very little about the attack on the Twin Towers. On their drive to visit Jim's mother's parents in another state, they had been rear-ended by an 18-wheeler. After the police left the accident scene, Jim's parents cancelled the trip, and called us after limping home in their badly-damaged car. We then guessed that the accident had occurred around the same time the second plane hit the World Trade Towers. Perhaps the truck driver had been distracted by the tragic, close-by, news.

There was nothing we could do to directly assist those in the two stricken cities, so we decided to go on with life as best we could. We found this to be helpful.

I tried to re-focus by looking at the family calendar. I confirmed by phone that the day's piano lessons had been cancelled, and I wondered if the school would still have its Open House on the 13th. Estimated taxes were due on the 17th. I needed to remember to finish working on them. Our church would have a much-needed prayer service at 7:00 pm.

We were not sure about the day's soccer practice,

but decided to go there and find out. At the soccer fields, people were slowly gathering. My son ran off to kick around a soccer ball with his friends. His coach was soldiering on, but could not help sharing with me her personal agony. She had two brothers-in-law who were missing. For one, it was his first day in a new job at the Pentagon. The second one worked at the Marriott Hotel at the base of the towers. No family member had received word from either of them.

After returning home, I again stared at the television. We were learning more about the hijackings, and what the people on board knew. Stories of those who had escaped the towers and damaged buildings nearby. The heroes on planes and in the buildings. We were inspired, and wondered if we would have acted so bravely. We hoped so.

September 12

On Wednesday morning, I pulled out a full-sized page of commemoration from our local newspaper, taping it to the end of the kitchen cabinet. It simply stated, "Never Forget. 9-11-2001." It would remain there for years.

We started putting out our American flag every day. We wanted to show respect for the dead, and hope for the future. The flag also represented solidarity with all who were suffering.

Finally, I was able to connect with my sister, who had an unexpected story about her whereabouts on 9/11. Through an unusual set of circumstances, as the attacks began she had been inside the Supreme Court building. She was in her workout clothes, taking a yoga class initiated by and including Justice Sandra Day O'Connor.

Following the class, my sister began walking home with a friend, still oblivious to the attacks. They heard what sounded like an explosion, coming from the proximity of the Capitol building. The noise turned out to be a sonic boom from a jet rapidly approaching to help protect the area. The husband of my sister's friend called them into the house, to watch the news coverage.

As my sister spoke with me, I realized that she likely would have perished if a hijacked plane had hit the relatively-small Supreme Court building, located across the street from the Capitol. Instantly, my appreciation increased exponentially for the brave passengers who had helped take down Flight 93, in Shanksville, PA.

My sister's husband had been working on an arbitration at his law office, a mere two blocks from the White House. His secretary interrupted to say that a plane had hit the Pentagon. First, everyone gathered around a television, and then they started returning home. My brother-in-law stayed at his office for a while, thinking that he might be at more risk on the Metro (i.e., the Washington underground train system) than remaining where he was. Both of their sons called to verify that he was safe. Throughout the entire ordeal, he and his wife trusted that the other was acting optimally, and that everything would be all right. Therefore, neither panicked.

Fortunately, after a few phone calls, I was able to track down our day-to-day contact at our Midtown-Manhattan business client. I discovered that he was safe, and had traveled to stay with his parents, who lived quite a distance from New York. He had first heard news of the crashes while at work. He then ran to the conference room, and could see the tops of the Towers burning in the distance. Stunned, he quickly left. Unfortunately, he lost a number of friends in the Towers.

In an emergency, doing something for someone else can help focus our minds on the positive. There is great satisfaction in helping, and our children knew this. They wanted to do something that mattered, so we discussed a number of options. In the end, they emptied their piggy banks, and we delivered the coins and wadded up bills to a local fire station. The firemen were greeting many donors, promising to pass the donations on to the fire houses in New York that had lost so many brave rescue workers.

There is one aspect of this time that can be easy to forget when looking back. No one knew what would happen next – or where. Other cities and potential targets prepared as best they could. All air traffic was grounded, with many people stranded far from those they loved. Would there be another attack? Our country collectively held its breath.

Time Reveals More Connections

Many stories came to light over time. For instance, the American Express building we visited in 1986 was badly damaged when the towers fell, but not destroyed. Other buildings close to the fallen towers could not be salvaged, and had to be torn down. Thankfully, there were no more attacks. However, our country was still on high alert, and would remain so for many weeks to come. My sister knew they were necessary, but became frustrated by new and plentiful barriers to public buildings in Washington, along with the constant hum of military aircraft overhead. She considered Washington to be her neighborhood, and she loved it more than ever.

Soon, my sister was back at the Supreme Court

building for another yoga session. Afterwards, she and her classmates joined many, if not all, of the Supreme Court Justices, in a large room. She was still in her yoga clothes, and a bit self-conscious. Everyone sang and prayed together, in a circle. They might have even held hands. I believe that the National Anthem was followed first by America The Beautiful and then by Amazing Grace. My sister, who passed away recently, had a wonderful voice. I can still picture, and almost hear, her singing with great strength and emotion.

My husband's brother-in-law was a police officer in Stamford, Connecticut, a nearby suburb of New York. He had jumped at the opportunity to help, volunteering to help ferry a number of police rescue boats to the downtown tip of Manhattan, where the towers had been. They docked near the wreckage, and unloaded massive quantities of ice and other supplies. He and his co-workers were given a tour of the rescue and recovery area. He was overcome by the immensity of the area, and the number of dedicated, determined searchers. The air was thick with smoke and debris. The rescuers who had run into certain danger on 9/11 made a difference, by getting people out of the buildings. Sadly, the number of rescues and recoveries after the towers fell was miniscule. My brother-in-law was forever changed.

One of my best and longest friends had a brother who worked at the Pentagon. His department was located where the plane hit the building on the west side, ripping it open and setting it ablaze. My friend was incredulous to discover that her brother, and only sibling, was unharmed. On September 11, his office had an off-site meeting, so the usual inhabitants had been spared.

A local friend's husband took an early flight on 9/11, traveling from Raleigh to Montana. In route, the flight was diverted to Madison, Wisconsin, for "mechanical reasons." As they deplaned, armed National Guard members lined the airport concourses, and passengers were directed to the main terminal. The one airport restaurant was blocked by a throng of passengers crowding around the televisions, seeing the news for the first time. Fortunately, her husband was able to connect with two other Raleigh passengers who were headed to the same destination: a man who had business in Montana and a young woman traveling to see her parents. The three got in separate car rental lines, which were all quite long. When one of them was able to get a car, the other two joined him and they drove to Montana together. By the time they arrived, they were no longer strangers.

An entrepreneurial couple at my church owned a business that designed trading floors for financial services companies tied to Wall Street. They also installed the custom trading desks and associated technical equipment. The husband and several employees were in One World Trade Center the day prior to the attack. They had been working at what proved to be the impact zone, just below Cantor-Fitzgerald, a company that was devastated by a direct hit to their offices on Floors 101 to 105. Fortunately, our friends' installation was not scheduled to continue in Tower One on 9/11, and they were working elsewhere in New York when the planes hit. The office under construction was empty.

A doctor living just around the corner from us was on a business trip in California. Because all planes in the U.S. were grounded for the foreseeable future, and rental cars and Amtrak sold out, she purchased a car and drove it across the country by herself. She had planned to buy a car soon, and was anxious to get home to her family and patients. Taking action was preferable to sitting and waiting in a faraway hotel room!

Fortunately, our son's soccer coach did not lose either of her two brothers-in-law, despite their proximity to danger in the Pentagon and Marriott. After many very anxious hours, each was able to contact family members, reassuring them, and telling them about harrowing escapes.

Friends from our years in Chicago were living abroad in Kosovo, working as English teachers. When news of the attack arrived, their small, predominantly Muslim city had a parade to honor this American family. The citizens wanted to assure these foreigners that there was nothing to fear from the community. And the locals wanted to show their appreciation for all the United States had done for them. Starting in March 1999, the U.S. had participated in a NATO military intervention to stop the genocide that had euphemistically been described as "ethnic cleansing." Our friends were incredulous, and grateful, for the powerful demonstration of support when they were so far from home.

Over time, it became apparent that just about everyone in the New York metropolitan area had been impacted. The ripple effect also affected me. Instead of traveling to New York later on in September, as scheduled, I used conferencing software for the first time. Also, a key vendor told me that she had lost her best friend, who had been at a breakfast meeting at Windows on the World.

Months later, when air travel was again possible, our Manhattan-based client came to our home for a meeting. We made sure to put out our family's American flag prior to his arrival. He was driven from the airport in a cab that was adorned with dozens of American flags. Some were on magnets, and others flapped in the wind as the vehicle pulled into our driveway. Before 9/11, we all would have thought the extreme display to be a bit overdone. However, our client deeply appreciated the sincerely-felt support for New York, and gave the driver a very generous tip. That taxi was a sight I have never forgotten.

Twenty Years Later

Many people, both Americans and non-Americans, had visited New York and Washington, D.C. before September 11, 2001 – as have many since that day. My family visited the Ground Zero New York site in 2003, when it was still a pile of rubble, cordoned off by a chain-link fence. Now, when I drive past the Pentagon, the building's scars have disappeared, but I still find myself looking for them. Shanksville, Pennsylvania welcomes pilgrims, and I look forward to being one of them. People want to visit these places, to remember and to mourn.

My sister's husband recently shared a story that remains quite moving to him, even after almost twenty years. On September 12, 2001, he was taking a run with the family dog around a nearby D.C. park. He greeted a man he often passed on his run, and they briefly acknowledged that life had changed. Understandable for any D.C. resident on that day, but there was more. Sadly, this neighbor's young granddaughter had been traveling with other youngsters to a spelling competition. They had been on the plane that had hit the Pentagon the previous day. She was simply…gone. Time does not erase a loss like that.

9/11 was the beginning of a long period of mourning for many. My personal sense of loss pales in comparison with the pain of people who were directly impacted, and I continue to remember them in prayer. People still grieve their losses, both personal and physical, as well as the loss of innocence for more than one generation. Many Americans had a hard time believing that such attacks could ever take place – until they actually did.

Our enemies underestimated the love that Americans have for their country. Not only the physical place, but the idea of who we are. The freedoms we cherish remain so rare in the world. We quickly galvanized as a single entity, and, for a time, overlooked our differences in a way that had not happened since World War II. We were hurt, and innocents had died, but we did our best to move forward – together.

Though physically far away, these events continue to touch me in very personal ways.

I will never forget.

*— **Cynthia B. Wheaton***

THE WORLD STILL REMEMBERS

September 11, 2003: This year brought us the birth of two new grandsons. Jacob was joined by his brother Zachary (March) and Cousin Kyle (September). Giving us two wonderful additions to our family. Unfortunately, my September 11th poem writing did not continue, but we did add another grandson, Austin, in 2007. My fears for their safety remain even as we approach the 20th anniversary of that horrific day. For many of us, it seems like yesterday and we still feel that overwhelming need to protect. September 11, 2001, will be a day we will never forget.

The World Still Remembers
2nd Anniversary

Zachary, my dearest, you are almost six months old,
Exploring your world and hearing stories
that are being told.
The horrific events of September 11th
happened two years ago today.
It's a sad reality that fear and war are here to stay.

When Jacob was your age, the world suddenly changed.
By some fanatical men who were certainly deranged.
They caused planes to crash in PA., New York,
and in D.C.
Terror shook the world since their actions we could see.

September 9th brought the birth of our beautiful Kyle,
We cherish his arrival and his cute little smile.
Dearest Grandsons you are the next generation
of young men.
We hope the world can recover
and horrible hatred will end.

The Pentagon and Twin Towers
have fallen in destruction
Crushing the dreams of millions,
so I give this instruction,
Your young lives are just beginning in this
crazy, mixed-up world.
It's upon you to be strong and love our flag
when it's unfurled.

The world will always remember
and mourn those who were lost.
We hope your world will be a better place
at not too great a cost.
Jake, Zach, and Kyle, my wish for you
as you grow older,
Is that peace reigns as you rest
your own baby's head on your shoulder.

P.S. It amazes me how many times remembrances of 9/11 have made an impact on my life. My first-born grandson Jacob, now twenty years old, has no recollection of that day and yet he was paired with a college roommate whose father died in the attack. His roommate is very knowledgeable of the events of 9/11 and only has a few baby pictures to remember a father he scarcely knew. He grew up in the New York City area and his step-father is a survivor of the attack, just barely having escaped the flames. Having this special roommate has made that day very real for Jacob not just a tragic event in history.

—Terry Hans

THE BURDENS OF 9/11

On 9/11/2001, a tragedy struck our nation. The impact of this tragedy was felt around the world because it not only affected our own citizens but people from sixty-one other countries.

After the immediate reaction of the day settled into concern about what our next steps would be as a country and how we would respond to this terrorist attack, I had time to absorb what had happened and felt compelled to write down my feelings about that day and the days that followed.

I wrote this poem on November 17, 2001, 67 days after 9/11, in honor of those who gave their lives and those who lost loved ones and those who continue to fight against terrorism, even today.

We tend to forget some of the things that happened in the months that followed—like the anthrax scares after 9/11 or hunting for the terrorists in caves—Bin Laden and others). And the passengers on flight 93? They did not hear their leaders' voices, but they did not need to; they took their orders from a higher power. They acted as one and gave their lives as Americans, as patriots and as heroes.

I felt burdened when I wrote this—but it gave me a welcome sense of perspective, as well.

I feel the burden of the hero—
of men between fire and falling,
flying and falling,
fighting and falling.

I feel the burden of the hunter—
of souls in wreckage,
men in caves,
clues in common life.

I feel the burden of the leaders—
who separated for safety,
joined for strength,
whose voice was not heard but whose will was done,
and the burden of a people stunned and sorrowful,
renaming fear and caution,
hope and justice.

— *Nancy Wakeley*

LOOKING BACK, LOOKING FORWARD

Where were you on 9/11? How did you react to the news?

Or if you weren't alive then, how do you think you would have reacted?

The contributors to this book have shared some very personal, very human stories. The reactions to the events of that momentous day were varied: shock, fear, anger and sadness combined with worry for the future and an intensified sense of patriotism and faith in God. Those who are old enough to remember still have some of these feelings about that day. But others have forgotten.

That day changed the whole country, indeed the whole world. The world we live in today is far different from twenty years ago. It's a more guarded, less trusting place on many fronts. Recent events, such as the Covid Pandemic, have changed it even further.

The story of 9/11 is an important story to tell, if only for the historical value. History is more than a series of dry dates and textbook events; it's the stories of individuals and how they react to the situations life has handed them.

We can learn much from those who have gone before us. We hope this book will help.

— Ellen Edwards Kennedy, Editor

OUR AUTHORS

While **Barbara Bennett**'s writings are typically humorous, the September 11th attacks will forever bring a lump to her throat. Her first published work, *Anchored Nowhere; A Navy Wife's Story*, traces her zany adventures around the world during 26 moves in 17 years. She has also had four stories published in the Chicken Soup for the Soul series. When not writing or spending time with her ever-growing family, she enjoys crafting and made over Anti-Covid masks for family and friends. E-mail her at **barbny2nc@gmail.com**

JoAnne Check is presently updating her historical fiction series, *Ella's World*, which is about family life in the 1880s in upstate New York. She was inspired to write about people's daily struggles and life experiences when conducting school tours at a restored 19th century village. In addition, she is a contributor to the *Chicken Soup for the Soul* series and has written her first novel, *My Friend, Mad Maddie*. She is a graduate of Kutztown University and has been a school teacher, grant writer, and copywriter. After living thirty years in New York, she and her husband now reside in Holly Springs, North Carolina. When JoAnne is not writing, she enjoys camping, gardening, and rainbow trout dinners. You can contact her at **www.joannecheck.com**

Emily Dykstra is a college student, who lives in Cary, North Carolina. She loves stories and has been creating them as long as she can remember. As a child, she asked her parents to tell her about things they did when they were little. Her hobbies include, but aren't limited to, blasting music so loud through her headphones that she'll probably wind up deaf before she's thirty, futilely reminding her werewolf characters that she is the boss not them, and procrastinating absolutely everything she needs to do until the last possible minute.

Terry Hans became inspired to write when she first heard the news of the impending birth of her first grandchild. She began writing poetry to celebrate each stage of his development. The poetry expanded to short stories and essays. Terry Hans has been published multiple times in the *Chicken Soup for the Soul* series. She is drawing on forty-five years as a Dental Hygienist to compile collection of Erma Bombeck-style humorous stories from her side of the hygienist's chair. Presently she is concentrating her efforts on this book she hopes to publish this year. Terry has two accomplished daughters, two incredible sons-in-law, and four athletic grandsons. Her passions are writing, scrapbooking and spending time with family. Most days you will find her and her husband cheering at one of their grandsons' sporting events.

Janet Harrison has been a member of CWC for about 7 years. She is working on a book about her experience hiking on the Appalachian Trail. Her short pieces portray the highlights of an outdoor girl who loves hiking, sailing, organic gardening, photography and just being outside. She has a passion for healthy living enhanced by the multitude of sustainable choices we each make every day.

Dea Irby: A Southerner who has lived throughout the south, Dea moved "north" to North Carolina in 2012 with her husband and the last of 8 children. She joined CAC in 2019. Dea is a contributing author to *From My Heart to Yours: Inspirational Messages from the Wives of Ministers* and two *Chicken Soup for the Soul* books. After owning and operating The Baron York Tea Room in North Georgia for 7 years, she published *A Dollop and A Pinch: Recipes and Stories from The Baron York*. She has published two books in a series of devotional journals – *An Ox in Your Kitchen: A Devotional Journal for Young Mothers* and *Like Dew on the Grass: A Devotional Journal for Women Seeking God*. Coming soon: a devotional journal for women in business. Dea, as a speaker, presents on her leadership strategy of building community to decrease attrition and increase the bottom line. To be published: *C.L.A.I.M. Your People*. Dea and her husband, Tom, form Irby Realty Group and serve the Research Triangle area of NC with Keller Williams. She enjoys working out at the gym and traveling all over the world to visit her 8 children and 18 grandchildren. (And, yes, she did get to go to Brazil for her grandson's birth.) For more info, visit her website: www.deairby. com. For an autographed copy of her cookbook email her at **deairby@gmail.com**

Ellen E. Kennedy, aka E.E. Kennedy, is an award-winning commercial copywriter and has lived in New York State, Alabama, Texas, and now North Carolina. She is the author of the Miss Prentice Cozy Mysteries: *Irregardless of Murder*, *Death Dangles a Participle*, *Murder in the Past Tense* and the award-winning *Incomplete Sentence*. She is the voice of "Gracie Gastank" for the Christian Car Guy Theater, syndicated on the Truth

Radio Network. She has been hosting the NC Scribes on a weekly basis for a little over eight years. She and her husband enjoy spoiling their five grandchildren in Fuquay Varina, NC.

James (Jim) Lewis was in law enforcement for thirty-six years where he spent twenty-five fun-filled years first as a beat officer, later as a vice-intelligence detective during which he spent some time undercover as a street person and concluded his career as a robbery and homicide detective. The next eleven years, he worked as a deputy sheriff with prisoners in the county court system. Jim was and always will be a proud marine. After retiring, he and his wife moved to North Carolina to spend time with their son, daughter-in-law, two beautiful granddaughters, and a sweet puppy named Lewie.

He has published two books that give the reader a ride-along look at life from the street side of police work. *Back in the Game* and *Death Upon a Midnight Clear* by Detective James Lewis can be found on Amazon. A third book in the series is almost ready to go to print.

Jim's email address is mongoose2633@yahoo.com and he is always willing to talk police work and tell stories.

Linda Loegel, now Linda Hemby, has lived all over this country, from as far north as Vermont, as far west as San Diego, as far east as Connecticut, and as far south as North Carolina. Now she prefers to sit on her back porch and watch the birds fly around. When she comes inside, her house is full of birds as well. She has three grown children and, at age eighty, became a newlywed, proof that it's never too late to find true love.

She has authored three nonfiction books: *If You Don't*

Like Worms, Keep Your Mouth Shut (a memoir about growing up in Vermont in the 1940s); *Bumps Along the Way* (a six-week, ten-thousand-mile, cross-country car trip); and *Stop Procrastinating—Get Published!* (a beginner's twelve-step guide to writing and getting published). She has also authored six historical fiction novels: *Willard Manor, Leaving Mark, Finding Gary, Saving Lou, Remaking Danny,* and *Redeeming Rob*. She is currently working on her seventh in the series. She has been published in *Guideposts, Chicken Soup for the Soul, Country Woman, Yesterday's Magazette, Good Old Days,* and *The Vermont Standard*. She is a member of the NC Scribes as well as a Thursday writing group in Garner, NC.

Karyn Mulligan is a native of upstate New York, growing up along the Niagara River. After graduating from Mercyhurst University with a degree in Social Work, she worked in Management before becoming a wife and mother, dedicating her time to home schooling. She now lives in Holly Springs, NC, with her husband and three grown children. She just published her first book, *Mess to Masterpiece*, a journal of recovery from childhood sexual abuse, over coming years of depression and anxiety. For the past two years she has served as a facilitator for MEND which provides help to women suffering from sexual trauma. Her ebook is available on Amazon, or contact her directly for a hard copy. **Karynm@reagan.com**. You may also contact her directly for speaking opportunities.

Nancy Panko is a retired pediatric RN and author of two award-winning novels: *Sheltering Angels and Guiding Missal—Fifty Years. Three Generations of Military*

Men. One Spirited Prayer Book. Panko is a sixteen-time contributor to *Chicken Soup for the Soul.* She has also been published in *Guidepost, Woman's World,* and *Cary Living* magazines, Nancy is a member of the NC Scribes, The Light of Carolina Christian Writers, and The Military Writers Society of America. She and her husband migrated from Lock Haven, Pennsylvania to Fuquay Varina, North Carolina in 2008 to live near their two children. They have four grandchildren and three granddogs. They love being in, on, or near the water of Lake Gaston with their family.

Laurie Winslow Sargent is an author formerly known for her parenting books, including *Delight in Your Child's Design* (on Kindle), inspirational stories in a dozen other books, and nonfiction magazine articles. She's now writing historical nonfiction and fiction based on true stories, intrigued and inspired by vintage documents from her own attic. Her current work-in-progress is based on the story of an American couple's expat experiences in the jungles and islands of British Raj India (1923-1933). Say hello to Lauric via her website and blog, at **www.LaurieSargent.com** or @LaurieSargent on Twitter.

Louise Edwards Sowa was born and raised in northern New York State. She is a graduate of Auburn University and the University of Alabama Law School, where she earned her JD. She has worked as a law clerk, a book editor, an adjutant English professor and an activities director for a retirement community. A member of Parker Memorial Baptist Church, Louise conducts regular Bible Studies in her apartment complex and teaches Sunday school. She is a widow, has one grown daughter and lives in Anniston, Alabama.

Maribeth Hynnes Stevens is a retired medical-surgical nurse. Now that she has retired, she is returning to her first love of writing. She had a column in Thornwood High School Newsletter, and was published in the high school writers publication until her family moved from Illinois to Louisiana. She received her Bachelor's degree in nursing from Northeast Louisiana University, and later a Master's of Divinity in Counseling from Southeastern Baptist Theological Seminary. Currently she volunteers with TWR Women of Hope at Trans World Radio in Cary, NC as a contributing writer to their newsletter. Her newest project is a devotional geared toward people with mental illness which she plans to have published in 2022. A newlywed, she lives with her caring, devoted husband Tom near Cary with their three rescue dogs and rescue cat who run the house. She enjoys gardening, camping, reading, cooking and exercising. She may be reached at **chaplainlady@gmail.com**

Kate Edwards Trussler is a strategist, a dreamer and a lover of puzzles and words. She is also a peddler of stories in the corporate arena, working in employee communications, human resources and higher education for the past twenty years. While she loves her day-to-day job and the unpredictability of the challenges it presents, her persistent aspiration is to work full-time as a novelist. Kate shares four children with her husband, and swears their dog likes her best.

Nancy Wakeley grew up in the New York State Finger Lakes region and now resides in Apex, North Carolina, with her husband. She completed her degree in health information management from Stephens College, Columbia, Missouri, and spent her career in the health information management and clinical research fields until the writing muse dictated retirement from Duke Clinical Research Institute. She belongs to the North Carolina Writer's Network, the Holly Springs Writers Guild and the CAC Writers Circle. She gives back to her community through volunteerism. She embraces all things fashioned out of musical notes and words as the ultimate reflection of life's exquisite journey. Heirloom is her debut novel, and she draws on personal experiences to express the journey through grief and healing. You can connect with her on Facebook at Nancy Wakeley and Author Nancy Wakeley, Instagram at nancywakeley2 and Twitter at @nancywakeley. "Heirloom (A Kate Tyler Novel)" can be purchased through Amazon.com or an autographed copy can be purchased from the author at **nancywakeley2@gmail.com**.

Cynthia Baughan Wheaton offers practical business advice, character encouragement and spiritual insight as The Entrepreneur's Friend®. She earned an MBA from The University of North Carolina at Chapel Hill at a time when few women sought one. Cynthia spent 9 years managing new ventures and then 25+ years as a business consultant, all while remaining very active in church and community. Cynthia and her husband nurtured their two children into purpose-driven adulthood while building their own successful business and working together from home. Her concise and readable book, *Are You Ready to Start Your Own Business? A Sanity Check for Those Who Dream of Self-Employment*, is currently used at two colleges. Her second book, *Make Your Home Office Work*, will be available in 2021. Find out more at **www.TheEntrepreneursFriend.com**.

Made in the USA
Middletown, DE
25 August 2021